The Satanic in Science Fiction and Fantasy

By A J Dalton

Academia Lunare

LUNA PRESS PUBLISHING

First published by Luna Press Publishing, Edinburgh, 2020

www.lunapresspublishing.com

ISBN-13: 978-1-913387-04-4

For Nadine West

Contents

1. Introduction

As long as literature has existed, so has the motif of the 'Dark Lord'. However, it was not until the emergence of science fiction and fantasy (SFF) as distinct literary genres that the Dark Lord truly became enshrined in popular works. From Bram Stoker's Dracula, to Tolkien's Sauron, to Donaldson's Lord Foul, to Lucas's Darth Vader, the Dark Lord was ever present in SFF. Sometimes he was a mad god, an evil emperor, or even an evil corporation, but always there was that malign intelligence seeking to thwart the goody-goody Chosen One, particularly in the works of the 1980s and 90s. He had servants in the form of demon armies, alien invaders or intelligent machines, seeking to drag the unwary into the underworld, to conquer us or to make humanity entirely extinct.

Come the new millennium, and the emergence of sub-genres like 'grimdark fantasy' and 'dystopian YA', we tend to see everything in shades of grey far more. We still have invading hordes, be they zombies or Dothraki, but they are mindless disease-carriers and immigrants-with-a-cause rather than out-and-out followers of Satan. Our sense of evil has perhaps changed. We seem to understand that 'evil' is really a matter of perspective. And what has become of the Dark Lord himself? Well, he is now the star of TV series such as *Lucifer* (2016) or *Dracula* (2013). Has he actually changed from anti-hero into hero? Has he won in some way?

Or do we now recognise ourselves in him? Were we really fighting against ourselves all along?

This book considers the early literary origins of the character of Satan and his embodiment within SFF, in order to show how our idea of evil has changed over time. To do so, this study will identify how SFF has shifted since its early days, to suggest the trends which are yet to emerge and, perhaps, to help us better understand ourselves.

Adam Dalton, Manchester, UK, April 2018

2. The literary origins of Satan

What is evil? Evil is evil, right? Even if you don't believe in absolute evil, you might imagine that we all have a pretty similar idea of what constitutes evil. It is true that those who share a particular culture are more likely to have a similar conception of wrong-doing, but that is not necessarily so. For example, an older generation British person might well hold 'traditional' views and values concerning sexual orientation, gender identity and 'correct' social behaviour (potentially considering anything that deviates from, subverts, transgresses or challenges those values and norms as 'evil'), while a younger person might be more liberal in their attitude towards such issues (and therefore not perceive 'evil' as inherent in alternative lifestyles). Statistically, an older generation person is more likely to possess Christian values, while a millennial is more likely to have post-Christian, pluralistic values[1].

Therefore, our definition of evil shifts and changes based

1. In 2016, the Church of England reported that the national congregation had fallen below one million people for the first time, and by 12% in a decade (Sherwood, 2016a). In the same year, NatCen's British Social Attitudes survey reported that 'the proportion of population who describe[d] themselves as Anglican had halved since 1983' and that '[t]he number of people who sa[id] they ha[d] no religion [wa]s escalating and significantly outweigh[ed] the Christian population in England and Wales' (Sherwood, 2016b).

on a whole range of factors. It depends upon individual perspective, cultural background and individual upbringing *but also* upon the major socio-historical events and moments of 'progress' that have helped inform our (Western) understanding of life and the world. The importance of such major socio-historical events and moments can most clearly be seen in how representations of Satan have changed during our history. The earliest depictions of him in the New Testament were as a braying horned beast who brought chaos, war and fiery suffering, precisely at a time when Saint Antipas, the Christian representative in the major city of Pergamon ('where Satan live[d]', according to the Book of Revelation), was being burnt alive within the hollow statue of a bull (a pagan effigy of Zeus). By contrast, the Satan of the Victorian era, a demonic Dracula, was a highly educated polyglot who was ultimately undone, in the eponymous novel, by means of the technology employed by those Englishmen hunting him: his pursuers used telegraph messages and trains to get ahead of the fleeing vampire and then, once they had him cornered, used hunting rifles to end things. Finally, the Satan of today's popular culture, be he the Darth Vader of the Star Wars franchise or the Lucifer of the TV series, is a sympathetic, often misunderstood and near tragic figure, a reflection of our modern preoccupations with self-awareness, self-knowledge, anxiety and being 'woke' (as described in more detail later in *The Satanic in Science Fiction and Fantasy*).

A close study of the history of Satan as a literary character thus allows us to understand the changing values and relationships of society. It also helps us understand how science fiction and fantasy are a reflection of, and direct comment upon, the moral, spiritual and philosophical condition and realities of their society. Without such an understanding and appreciation of Satan and SFF, I would argue, we are far lesser readers and far lesser individuals.

2.1 The Dark Lord and the white knight

It may surprise some to learn that Satan does not appear as a personification of evil in the Old Testament (OT) of the Bible (c.400BC). The serpent in the Garden of Eden is never named as Satan or described as any sort of supernatural entity. Indeed, rather than being a character's name, the original Hebrew term 'satan' is a generic noun meaning 'adversary' (Kelly, 2006). Of the 27 uses of this noun in the OT, 17 of them are entirely generic/non-specific references to 'the satan' (it is unclear whether the agency is angelic, human or otherwise), seven more refer specifically to human beings, and two (including 2 Samuel 24) refer to an Angel of Yaweh acting on God's behalf. The remaining reference in 1 Chron 21 simply references 'a satan' in a repeat of the story (told in Samuel) of David being punished by the Angel of Yaweh.

If we get any sense at all of Satan as a single, named character from the OT, it is as an angel of God's celestial court carrying out the sacred tasks of God's will. Far from being banished to some burning hell, Satan is one of heaven's glorious representatives, honoured with the role of testing the worthiness of humans and punishing transgressors. Satan, therefore, acts as a divine prosecutor, only 'adversarial' in that he is an advocate of divine-will-as-the-law.

It is not until the New Testament (NT), approximately five hundred years later, that we have Satan as the distinct and named 'devil' with which modern audiences will be more familiar. This later version of Satan is diametrically opposed to the will of God, is as monstrous as it is seductive, represents sin in all its guises and only has a malign intent towards humankind.

With the increased characterisation of Satan's nature in the NT, we also have an increased amount of description of his physical manifestation(s). It is the NT that claims the serpent in the OT's Garden of Eden to be one of Satan's avatars, and he is also described variously as 'an enormous red dragon with seven heads and ten horns and seven crowns', 'a dragon that can spew water like a river', 'the beast', a demon who can possess humans, one who can mark the heads and hands of his followers and 'a thorn in the flesh' (Biblica, 1978).

Therefore, the move from OT to NT sees Satan go from holy agent to a being who is entirely demonic in both behaviour and appearance. We must wonder what has happened in the five hundred years between the writing of the OT and NT to cause this ideological shift in representation. A closer examination reveals that the NT makes certain telling references and gives us some clues. In the Book of Revelation, Jesus instructs John of Patmos:

> 'To the angel of the church in Pergamon write:
> These are the words of him who has the sharp, double-edged sword. I know where you live – where Satan has his throne. Yet you remain true to my name. You did not renounce your faith in me, not even in the days of Antipas, my faithful witness, who was put to death in your city – where Satan lives.
> (Biblica, Revelation 2: 12-13)

It appears that particular problems had occurred for the Christian faith in the city of Pergamon, and that these problems were due to an evil intent or ethos personified in Satan. By understanding what happened to the Christian priest Antipas, and the politics surrounding his death, we will see that the character of Satan was actually used to 'demonise' all those who were not Christian. This construction of Satan, then, was the product of the Christian faith engaging in a form of caricature-based political propaganda.

Pergamon was an ancient Greek city in what is now eastern Turkey. During the time of Antipas, who was executed in 92AD, the city was governed by Rome and was a regional and political capital. It was the site of one of Christianity's seven major churches in Asia Minor, but also had major temples dedicated to the Greco-Egyptian god Serapis (Osiris twinned with Apis), to Athena twinned with Zeus, as well as to several other Greco-Roman gods and even to the Roman emperor himself. The city was also home to a famous school of medicine (where the renowned Greek doctor Galen himself practised) dedicated to the god of healing Asclepius, whose symbol was the snake. Purportedly, Antipas, whose name translates as 'against all', was killed by pagan priests and the followers of Serapis for refusing, when tested, to declare the Roman emperor as 'lord and god' above all (Renner, 2010). The manner of Antipas's death is well documented: he was placed inside a life-size metal statue of a bull (the Brazen Bull had been previously gifted to the city by King Attalus, 241-197BC) and a fire was set beneath it; the screams of his death would have echoed inside the statue and sounded as if the bull was bellowing; the god was thereby brought to 'life' by the human sacrifice. Scholars such as Renner (2010) believe that the Brazen Bull would have been located upon the Great Altar of Zeus (the throne of Satan mentioned in Revelation) – an altar which took the form of a magnificent set of marble stairs and colonnades surrounded by a frieze of the Gigantomachy[2] (the battle between the Giants and the Olympian gods for supremacy of the cosmos) – atop the acropolis of Pergamon. From there, the public execution could be better seen and heard by all those in the city.

With Pergamon described as the home of Satan, its temples described as Satan's throne, and the murderous attack on the priest of Christianity representing the action by which the devil 'lives', Satan becomes the personification of all pagan or non-Christian religions and all physical and political attacks upon Christianity. He is synonymous with bloody sacrifice, scheming, false idols, lies, cunning tests, death and brutality, fire and screaming, the animalistic, and a struggle for dominance and dominion. In terms of physical representation, he takes on the horns of a bull and the forked tongue of a snake. References to the bull might come from Apis the bull god, Zeus as a bull, or the golden calf of Exodus. The forked tongue of the snake, on the other hand, might relate to Asclepius (whose healers interfered with God's will by way of their arcane arts), or the snake upon the god statue at the temple of Serapis as the Egyptian symbol of rulership and power, or yet again the snake in the Garden of Eden, or the ancient serpent that is the dragon. Finally, we see that the place over which he presides is a place of horror, torture, unholy spectacle and the public witnessing, endorsement or celebration of both sinful and sacrilegious acts. It is the exact opposite of the Kingdom of Heaven; it is literally hell-on-earth. It is not a place of 'light' (for Jesus is 'the light of the world', in John 8); rather, it is a place of darkness and the fires of punishment.

Pergamon is also a vision of what Satan wants for all of

---

2. In the 19th century, the Great Altar was taken to Berlin and put on permanent display in the city's Pergamon Museum in 1930, just in time to inspire the dark cult of Nazism.

humankind and all of the earth; it is his political ambition, ideology and violent desire. He seeks to prevent heaven-on-earth, by establishing his own throne on earth and violently overseeing some hell or dark underworld. Indeed, the Osiris aspect of Serapis was god of the dead and ruler of the underworld, depicted by the god statue at the temple of Serapis in Pergamon as Hades with Cerebus/Anubis sitting at his feet. Just as Satan is differently depicted in the NT compared with the OT, then, so this NT version of 'hell' is a distinctly different one compared to what was meant by hell in the OT. The word 'hell' appears 31 times in the OT, each time translated from the Hebrew word 'sheol', a word that – unlike the English word 'hell' – has no connotation as a place of punishment. The word 'sheol' refers more generally to a place of the dead, a place that has a section for the 'righteous' dead and a separate section for the non-righteous. Indeed, the concept of sheol is more akin to the ancient Greek concept of an underworld (with its Elysian fields and Dys) than to anything else (McPherson, 2001-13).

Consequently, we begin to understand Satan and his acts as both a metaphorical personification and actual description of the physical and political persecution that Christians were suffering during the extended period of the NT's writing. Just as the nature of that persecution of and the opposition to Christianity changes with time, so the qualities of Satan shift and expand so that all anti-Christian acts may be included. Ultimately, Satan must come to be the antagonist (the Dark Lord) set against everything that Christianity represents, and must perform the attempt to bring down heaven itself to replace God the King in some sort of military coup. Thus, the dramatic climax or the 'story' of the war in heaven at the end of the Bible (Revelation), when Satan attempts a coup, is logically inevitable:

> Then war broke out in heaven, Michael and his angels
> fought against the dragon, and the dragon and his angels
> fought back. But he was not strong enough, and they lost
> their place in heaven. The great dragon was hurled down
> – that ancient serpent called the devil, or Satan, who leads
> the whole world astray. He was hurled to the earth and his
> angels with him.
> (Biblica, Revelation 12)

As we have seen, having been hurled down to the earth,
Satan made his home in the city of Pergamon, turning that
city into the place of 'dark' torture and moral ruination
that Satan sought to visit upon heaven's shining 'city'
(Matthew 5). Yet, Pergamon was more than just a city: it
was a centre for the pre-Christian Roman Empire, and it
worshipped the Roman Emperor in a number of temples.
The pre-Christian Roman emperors, therefore, particularly
those who persecuted Christians (and saw to Jesus being
sent to his death), are effectively agents of Satan, or Satan
himself, presiding over a dark and evil empire. The ambition
of such agents and agency is/was to extinguish Christianity
throughout the world of Man, and to rule the human earth
entirely.

Naturally enough, the Bible cannot allow or afford to
have Satan continuing to rule or thriving in Pergamon or
anywhere else. The will of God has to be seen as ultimately
prevailing. As the NT was completed in c.120AD,
approximately two hundred years *before* the Roman Empire
converted to Christianity, the writers and compilers of the
Bible were faced with a particular 'creative' difficulty since,
at that time, Pergamon was still ruled by its Satanic Roman
emperor. The only way out of that difficulty, of course, was
for there to be a vision (or prophecy) of the future in the
book of Revelation, a vision in which we see Satan defeated

once more, this time once and for all. There has to be a final, climactic, all-consuming battle, with the complete annihilation of the enemy, thus eliminating any possible threat thereafter. In short, there must be an end of days and an end to all possibility of human sin. Inevitably, the earth as it currently is must end, with the Kingdom of Heaven triumphing over all.

I saw heaven standing open and there before me was a white horse, whose rider is called Faithful and True. With justice he judges and wages war. […] He is dressed in a robe dipped in blood, and his name is the Word of God. The armies of heaven were following him, riding on white horses and dressed in fine linen, white and clean. Coming out of his mouth is a sharp sword with which to strike down the nations. "He will rule them with an iron scepter." He treads the winepress of the fury of the wrath of God Almighty. […] Then I saw the beast and the kings of the earth and their armies gathered together to wage war against the rider on the horse and his army. But the beast was captured, and with it the false prophet who had performed the signs on its behalf. With these signs he had deluded those who had received the mark of the beast and worshiped its image. The two of them were thrown alive into the fiery lake of burning sulfur. The rest were killed with the sword coming out of the mouth of the rider on the horse, and all the birds gorged themselves on their flesh. […] And I saw an angel coming down out of heaven, having the key to the Abyss and holding in his hand a great chain. He seized the dragon, that ancient serpent, who is the devil, or Satan, and bound him for a thousand years. He threw him into the Abyss, and locked and sealed it over him, to keep him from deceiving the nations anymore until the thousand years were ended. After that, he must be set

free for a short time. [...] Then I saw "a new heaven and a new earth," for the first heaven and the first earth had passed away, and there was no longer any sea. I saw the Holy City, the new Jerusalem, coming down out of heaven from God, prepared as a bride beautifully dressed for her husband. And I heard a loud voice from the throne saying, "Look! God's dwelling place is now among the people, and he will dwell with them. They will be his people, and God himself will be with them and be their God.
(Biblica, Revelation 19-21)

It is from the Bible, then, that we not only get the character of Satan as the Dark Lord, but also the character of the heavenly warrior as a virtuous knight upon a white horse. And this knight fights the dragon and defeats it. Surely, we are put in mind of the later character of St George, who similarly defeats the 'dragon of the abyss', a dragon who (according to the seventh century hagiography of St George (Société des Bollandistes, 1895)) is a monarch that persecuted the saint for his Christianity. Historically, St George (c.256-303AD) was a Roman officer-soldier of Greek origin called Georgius. He was a Christian and was martyred (on 23 April) in eastern Asia Minor by Emperor Diocletian, for not recanting his faith.

There are strong echoes of the persecution of Antipas in Pergamon in the life story of St George. However, where the bloody and sacrificial death of Antipas served to personify, celebrate and witness that Dark Lord who is Satan, the stoic death of Georgius served to inspire witnesses to convert to Christianity, to see him beatified and to see the dragon ultimately defeated. Less than a decade after Georgius's martyrdom, in 313AD Emperor Constantine issued the Edict of Milan and Christianity quickly became the official religion of the Roman Empire. It is at this point that Satan's dark empire is overthrown, the holy Roman Empire begins, and Rome becomes the 'holy city' (Revelation 21) at the centre of God's new kingdom on earth.

It is for the above reasons that St George became a patron saint in England, Georgia (the country named after him, where the first medieval account of St George fighting a physical, rather than metaphorical, dragon was written), and 22 other countries. It is why he is venerated in Anglicanism, Eastern Orthodoxy, Lutheranism, Oriental Orthodoxy, Roman Catholicism and Umbanda. It is why there are chapels and places of worship dedicated to him around the world. And it is why this soldier-saint became the symbolic figurehead of the Christian crusades, Rome's attempt to claim Jerusalem for Christianity. For Christian soldiers, bravery, suffering and sacrifice would see Christianity defeat the dragon and save the kingdom from its fire and torment forever. Success in Jerusalem would see the entire known world brought within Christianity, and Satan's own ministry and kingdom put to an end. The earth as it was would be ended and Jerusalem would be the 'new Jerusalem' of Revelation 21, when the earth would be a heaven and all those who had given their lives would live in the eternal city and kingdom.

For the writers, editors and compilers of the Christian Bible, the white knight who defeats the Dark Lord in a climactic battle, thereby seeing the kingdom of earth saved and made a paradise (the Kingdom of Heaven), was dramatically satisfying, powerful political propaganda, a persuasive mix of historical fact and prophetic fiction, and ideologically coherent, compelling and complete. It was a masterpiece in thematic, creative and even literary terms.[3] For the newly-Christianised Rome, its subsequent popes and soldiery, the Bible was an inspiring historical narrative, a

3. Indeed, it is a towering work in the shadow of which we still work, live and write.

political manifesto, a mission statement, a visionary guide for self-improving day-to-day conduct, legal and moral justification for the Christianising of Rome, legitimacy for all Church-sanctioned actions, and a contract with a priceless reward-upon-completion. As a result, Pope Urban II understood the Bible's description of Satan being chained in the abyss for a thousand years (Revelation 20) as literal. He understood the warning '[Satan] could not fool the nations anymore until 1000 years were completed' and 'After this he must be free a while' as an all-too-real clear-and-present-danger, and as a literal instruction to act without delay once the thousand years were up. Therefore, precisely a thousand years after the writing of the Book of Revelation, Pope Urban II launched the first crusade to 'free' Jerusalem, in 1095 A.D. His soldiers had St George (upon 'a white horse') as their figurehead and rallying cry, they wore the 'fine linen, white and clean' and the red cross of 'a robe dipped in blood' (as described in Revelation 19-21), and they were considered the actual holy army of the Bible's white knight 'called Faithful and True'. This was no metaphor. Fantasy and reality, history and the future, the physical and the spiritual, mortal life and eternity were all one and the same. Thus, at the time of the crusade, Satan was considered real and loose in the world, along with his numerous agents.

2.2 The princess-bride and the demon-queen

Naturally, it was around the time of the first crusade that the legend of St George and the Dragon became most popular and current. Icons and images started to proliferate as a vivid and visual retelling of the Bible narrative that would reach the illiterate and those who had no direct access to the text of the Bible. The legend served as dehumanising propaganda concerning the alien, bestial, dark-skinned and lowly enemy, and it readily lent itself to shifts in symbology so that it could be tailored or personalised to the soldiery and customs of the different nations of Christendom. By way of example, there are two obvious shifts in the telling or depiction of the legend. First, the dragon is sometimes instead portrayed as a giant snake, better understood by those of a Greco-Roman culture and tradition, as per the cruel pagan gods of Pergamon previously mentioned. Second, the green-hilled kingdom that is being saved is sometimes instead portrayed as a princess-bride suffering the lascivious and rapine attentions of a sexualised dragon (complete with penetrative barbed tail, overbright eye and extended forked tongue).

Tellingly, the figure of the princess-bride does not exist in the original Georgian text or visual depictions of the legend (10th-11th cent.), but she is quickly introduced to the Latin versions that circulated in France and England during the 12th and 13th centuries.(Jacobus de Voragine's *The Golden Legend*, c.1260, and Vincent de Beauvais's *Speculum Historiale*, at about the same time, just two of many examples). The figure of the princess-bride of course performs a range of symbolic and propagandist functions: she humanises the quest to free Jerusalem, just as the dragon dehumanises the enemy; she represents a more personal promise of reward and motivation for the crusaders than the simple claiming of foreign hills. With St George defending her honour (as per the medieval traditions of 'courtly love'), she enables the representation of a moral and superior set of behaviours that justify and legitimate the destruction of the enemy, while romanticising, spiritualising and validating the male struggle and sacrifice the crusaders must endure in order to see her protected and enshrined in a blessed future. These functions are entirely understood in Jacobus de Voragine's *The Golden Legend*, for the confrontation is replete with both religious and psycho-sexual imagery. At first, the princess-bride tries to send St George away, so that he might be spared and to show she is not one to 'court' others for selfish gain, to show that she is an 'honest' woman. Then the venom-spewing dragon emerges from the nearby pool, intent on having the princess-bride, St George makes the sign of the cross and charges on horseback, wounding the dragon with his 'lance'. He calls for the princess-bride to throw him her 'girdle' and he loops it around the dragon's neck, so that it will follow her as a 'meek beast' upon a leash. They lead the dragon to the city and St George offers to kill the dragon upon condition the terrified King and people convert to Christianity, which they duly do. Upon the spot where St George slays the dragon, the King then builds a church to the Virgin Mary, and a spring flows from its altar with water that cures all the disease originally caused by the dragon's venom.

It is from this version of the St George legend, which can be interpreted as another version of the Book of Revelation chapters 19-21, that the character of Satan is first furnished with the particularly venal and carnal ambitions with which modern audiences are familiar, those Satanic desires that inevitably tempt and corrupt humankind. In the Book of Revelation, 'the Whore' of Babylon is largely synonymous with Satan, but she does not possess the sexually proactive and predatory qualities that are exhibited by the dragon in *The Golden Legend*. It is the latter narrative, then, that represents the full sexualisation of Satan, the moment when audiences begin to think of hell as potentially being full of all sorts of sexual degradation, decadence and perversion. This characterisation adds to the image of Satan as some sort of Great Seducer testing and tempting us towards our own doom. At the same time, this construction of Satan invests him with a greater physicality than previously, making him even more real, and making immediate one of the ways in which he seeks to possess us and make his desires our own desires. More than that, we come to understand even better how he also has shape-changing abilities, for is he not able to adopt any form or gender with which to seduce us most? He could be anyone around us, which is a terrifying thought, one that can only inspire greater faith.

It is in this moment (albeit not for the first time) that sex itself becomes more demonised within Western European culture, and its sinful nature is reaffirmed as a defining aspect of Christian doctrine, policy, behaviour, judgement and censure. Indeed, it was in the Middle Ages that celibacy among Catholic priests truly became widespread, none of the Popes between 1003 A.D. and 1265 A.D. being married, unlike in the preceding and following periods. This ideological assertion allowed the Church to exercise an even greater controlling power over the individual: for sexual instinct, personal desire and even private thoughts and actions were placed (via confession) within a framework of moral, social and legal judgement, and sexual congress could only take place within the Church-controlled sacrament of marriage. More than that, our very bodies and minds (in being desirous of the sexual act) were made sinful, or sin-made-flesh, and in need of the ministrations of the Church. Thereby, Satan became even more real, because he was in us and a part of us. Sexual desire became his tempting words in our minds and the sexual act became him possessing our bodies. Hence, we have the tradition that he could only be cast out by a flagellation of the flesh or an exorcism performed by a priest.

Through this demonising of sex (sexual corruption), the committing of 'original sin' was no longer regarded as Adam and Eve simply stealing the forbidden fruit of knowledge:

now it was Eve seducing Adam with sexual knowledge of a penile snake; their shame no longer concerned the theft, but rather their nakedness. Through this demonization of sex, the 'fall' of man (and the Roman Empire) during the pre-Christian era was now perceived as being synonymous with a time of Roman orgies, sexual decadence and festivals (like the Saturnalia) dedicated to pagan gods (like Venus, Bacchus and Pan) who were celebrated and worshipped via acts of sexual depravity and promiscuity.

Unfortunately, it was also through this demonization of sex that, as per a homo- or heteronormative patriarchy and Eve's seduction of Adam, women and female sexuality became particular agents and an agency of Satan. Thus, the concept of the *succubus* (female demon) was born. According to the Zohar, a foundational work of Jewish mystical thought (Roth, 1971) which first appeared in thirteenth century Spain, published by the Jewish writer Moses de Leon, Adam's first wife was Lilith, and she left the Garden of Eden to mate with the archangel Samael (read as Satan) and be transformed into a succubus and queen of demons. Indeed, Geoffrey Chaucer's *Troilus and Criseyde* (c.1380) describes a similarly demonising and implicitly misogynist narrative in its final part, called 'The Betrayal' (Kline, 2018b, v. 30):

[H]e cursed Jove, Apollo and Cupid, ay,/ cursed Ceres, Bacchus and Venus beside,/ his birth himself, his fate, and even nature/ and, save his lady, every other creature./ […] To bed he goes, and tosses there and turns/ in fury, as does Ixion in hell./ […] God knows I thought, O lady bright, Cressid,/ that every word was gospel that you said./ But who can better beguile us when they must,/ than those in whom men place their greatest trust? […] And when he was slain in this manner,/ his light ghost full blissfully went/

up to the hollowness of the eighth sphere,/ leaving behind every element./ And there he saw, clear in his ascent,/ the wandering planets, hearing harmony/ in sounds full of heavenly melody./ [...] Such ending has Troilus, lo, through love:/ such ending has all his great worthiness,/ such ending has his royal estate above,/ such ending his desire, his nobleness,/ such ending has false words' fickleness./ And thus began his loving of Cressid,/ and in this way he died, as I have said./ [...] And love Him, who truly out of love/ on a cross, to redeem our souls that day,/ first died, then rose, to sit in heaven above:/ for he deceives no one, I say,/ who his heart shall wholly on him lay./ And since He is best to love, and most meek,/ what need is there for feigned loves to seek?

Where Troilus is constant and faithful in his love, Criseyde is fickle, false and traitorous (in a dream, Troilus is shown Criseyde sleeping with the enemy). In addition, her love is as feigned as she is 'beguil'ing' and 'deceit'ful', leading Troilus towards a 'hell' of suffering. For remaining faithful, Troilus is in the end rewarded with an ascent to heaven and compared to Christ; although we are not explicitly told what happens to Criseyde, the dualistic oppositions of the text make it clear her 'guilt' (v.254) and 'fallen' nature will see her consigned to hell. Although Chaucer asserts he does not wish to give all women a bad name (v.254), the examples of virtuous women he refers to are Penelope (who would have chosen a new 'husband' and king for herself had Odysseus not arrived home from the Trojan War at the necessary moment in the plot) and Alceste (who would have chosen a new 'husband' for herself but for Apollo's intercession). Ultimately, the dualistic oppositions of good and evil, spiritual virtue and physical corruption, Christ and Satan,

constancy and inconstancy, truth and falsity, generosity and
spite, the Christian and non-Christian, and even heaven and
hell, all map onto the patriarchal and heteronormative binary
of male and female. All virtue, nobility and worthiness as
they are displayed in *Troilus and Criseyde* are male, be
it on the battlefield or in social relationships. It is in this
Chaucerian work that the real, physical and suborning
capacity of Satan acting through female sexuality and the
feminine is truly spelt out.

Mapping the basic opposition of good and evil onto male
and female might have worked within the simple before-
and-after plot of the melodramatic, stylised, non-realist and
anachronistic 'courtly romance' that is *Troilus and Criseyde*,
but it seriously limited the work's ability to be relevant
for, reflect and engage a wider society, particularly one in
which the Church preached that sin existed in all of us, not
just in the female, and that the Mother Mary was free of
sin (even sexual sin, thanks to the concept of 'immaculate
conception'). Besides, a heteronormative patriarchy cannot
remain comfortable with the notion that all intercourse with
the female is simply intercourse with the shape-shifting
but male Satan, since this implies some sort of latent or
vicarious homosexuality. It is not so surprising then that as
a counterpoint to the more immature work of *Troilus and
Criseyde* (c.1380), Chaucer later produces *The Legend
of Good Women* (c.1385-87), in which he is reprimanded
by the god of love and his own queen for having depicted
women in a bad light and is ordered to write a poem extolling
female virtues as a 'penance', in an attitude that anticipates
the more contemporary, diverse and socially expansive *The
Canterbury Tales* (c.1387-1400).

Unlike in *Troilus and Criseyde*, in Chaucer's greater
work the figure of the virtuous princess-bride is presented in
a good number of tales as a positive example of femininity.

Indeed, the princess in 'The Man of Law's Tale' is allegorically named Constance, and she successfully prays to Mother Mary on two occasions for salvation. However, as might be expected of a heteronormative patriarchy, this figure is always defined by virtue of her chastity or sexual abstinence – meaning she is sexually disempowered – and usually placed within a victim-of-circumstance plot. Be it Constance in 'The Man of Law's Tale', the tragic virgin in 'The Physician's Tale', the faithful widow in 'The Friar's Tale' or the chaste Emilie in 'The Knight's Tale', the female character always needs to be saved or won by a divine or male agency. Also, we are frequently reminded that females are just as often 'the devil's very own officers' (l. 18), as they are termed in *The Pardoner's Tale*, or Satan in disguise, as per 'The Man of Law's Tale' (v. 33):

O serpent masked in femininity/ Like the serpent who in hell is bound!/ O feigning woman, all that may confound/ Virtue and innocence, through your malice,/ Is bred in you, the rest of every vice!/ O Satan, envious since that day/ When you were chased from our heritage/ You know well woman's ancient way!/ You made Eve bring us into bondage./ You will foredoom this Christian marriage./ Your instrument – well-away the while! –/ You make of woman, whom you will beguile.

Another major difference between *Troilus and Criseyde* and *The Canterbury Tales*, however, is that the latter sets out to describe the nature and diversity of 'male' sin. In all the tales that contain the figure of the princess-bride, the female is beset, socially manipulated or physically threatened by 'lecherous' males seeking to possess her sexually or otherwise take advantage of her. For example, in 'The Man of Law's Tale', the Sultan of Syria fakes his own conversion from Islam to Christianity and lobbies the Pope just so that he might 'have' the unwitting Princess Constance of Rome. Satan, then, causes a young knight to 'love her so hotly, with [such] a foul affection' (Part 2, v. 29) that when spurned he frames her for murder. After this, a 'heathen' lord's steward is intent upon raping her until blessed Mary tips him off a boat to drown him. Virginia, in 'The Physician's Tale', ultimately dies of shame because the Governor sees her and 'Anon the devil into his heart now ran' to start a scheme by which he might corrupt and have her. In 'The Friar's Tale', we are told of a summoner who 'spares the lechers' (v. 2), falls in with his 'brother' (v. 11) the devil, while commenting 'You have a man's shape as well as me' (v. 17), and becomes unstuck when trying to entrap a faithful widow.

What we can also see in the above examples is that, with *The Canterbury Tales*, when males do sin sexually it is because Satan has directly made them do so, by entering their hearts or causing their minds to 'darken', or indirectly made them do so through 'irresistible' women. It seems that when they are sinning, then, males are victims of Satan, whereas females are acting on Satan's behalf.

Or so it would seem. Because then we have 'The Wife of Bath's Tale', in which the 'female' is finally presented as a fully-rounded character in her own right rather than just an object of male temptation or cypher for male sin. Significantly, 'The Wife of Bath's Prologue' and tale were written later than the tales previously mentioned, and just after the death of Chaucer's wife in 1387. Furthermore, the tale's theme of a rapist-knight looking to atone for his crime via a quest to ascertain how to make a woman happy very much seems to represent Chaucer's own 'penance' for the rape of Cecilia Chaumpaigne (of which he was accused in 1380) and for the general treatment of women in both his life and writing.

It is important to note that, unlike with the majority of the characters in *The Canterbury Tales*, 'The Wife of Bath's Prologue' is longer (twice as long, in fact) than the tale itself. Thus, the Wife of Bath's section of *The Canterbury Tales* is more about her female character her and the 'modern' world in which she lives than it is about some classical tale, abstract moral lesson or hypocritical religious stricture concerning behaviour. Indeed, the old woman looking for love in the actual tale is in the self-same position as the Wife of Bath, so the tale itself only serves to describe the Wife and comment upon (perhaps satirise) the society of her times.

At the beginning of the her prologue, it is tempting to see the Wife, who has outlived five husbands and is now looking to 'purchase' the services of a young and hot-blooded sixth, as an overblown or larger-than-life character, as a grotesque caricature of a lewd, shockingly inappropriate and sexually-monstrous woman whom we should mock or scorn, as the Lilith or 'demon-queen' type that we find in 'The Man of Law's Tale' when we are presented with the jealous and murderous Islamic mother of the Sultan. It is tempting to consider her quick wit, emotional intelligence and insightfulness as tricks and weapons with which she seeks to seduce or engage us in order to lead us towards personal sin and some sort of social Saturnalia. However, as previously mentioned, the Wife is then revealed to be a far more rounded character than that. Indeed, it is the Wife herself who describes the dualistic, reductive and undermining oppositions and mechanism by which the patriarchy traditionally describes, defines and socially controls women (v. 13):

You tell me, then, how it's a great mischief/ To wed a poor woman, the expense./ And then if she's rich, of good descent,/ Then you say it's a torment and misery/ To endure her pride and melancholy./ And if she be fair, you proper knave/ You say that every lecher has his way/ With her, since none in chastity abide,/ When they are assailed from every side.

In hearing how the Wife has been mistreated by men, from the age of twelve no less, we develop an understanding of her as a victim and realise that her manner, which has initially appalled us, is the result of what men have done to her. We come to realise that she is not looking for a new husband for some sexually predatory reason after all, but simply because she is still looking for a 'good' man, a gentle companion and helpmate rather than a cruel rapist and robber. It dawns on us that she is lonely and desperate for some sort of genuine love or, failing true love, then some basic human affection. The Wife is in her later years, slightly overweight and has lost the good looks of her youth. She is terrified of dying alone and unloved. We empathise with her on a fundamental human level… and then we come to respect and admire her, for she refuses to let us pity her. Her ribald humour, her knowing nudges and winks, her outrageous flouting of social convention, her sexually frank comments, her satirical observations, her borderline blasphemy and her lurid exaggeration of her life-story put us through just about every emotion… except pity. We know it's all an act, but it's one that is as entertaining as it is distracting. We love her for it, for she is seeking to spare us the tragedy and heartache that she has suffered. She is a strong woman, a powerful woman. She is worldly wise but still emotionally generous, compassionate and optimistic, even after all that has happened to her. Despite all her noise and theatrics, there are a great dignity and quiet tragedy about her.

'Choose now,' quoth she, 'which of these to try:/ To see me old and ugly till I die,/ And be to you a true and humble wife,/ Who never will displease you all my life,/ Or else you may have me young and fair,/ And take the risk that all those who repair/ To our house are there because of me,/ And to other places, it well may be./ Now choose, yourself, just as you like.'/ The knight thought deeply and with a sigh/ At last he replied to her in this manner:/ 'My lady and my love, and wife so dear,/ I place myself in your wise governance./ Choose yourself which is the most pleasant,/ And brings most honour to me and you./ I do not care which it is of the two,/ For as you like it, that suffices me.'/ 'Then have I won the mastery,' quoth she,/ 'Since I may choose and govern as I wish?'/ 'Yes, surely, wife,' quoth he, 'I hold that best.'/ 'Kiss me,' quoth she, 'and no more wrath./ For, by my troth, I to you will be both –/ That is to say, both fair and good./ I pray to God I shall die mad, and would,/ If I be not to you both good and true/ As ever wife was, since the world was new./ And if I be not tomorrow as fair to see/ As any lady, Empress or Queen may be,/ Who lives between the east and the west,/ Do what you wish touching my life and death./ Lift the curtain; see what already is.'/ And when the knight swiftly saw all this,/ That she was young, and lovely too,/ For joy he took her in his arms two./ His heart was bathed in a bath of bliss;/ A thousand times in a row they kiss,/ And she obeyed him in everything/ That pleased him and was to his liking./ And thus they lived to their lives end/ In perfect joy – and Jesus Christ us send/ Husbands meek, young, and fresh abed,/ And grace to outlive those that we wed./ And also I pray Jesus, trim the lives/ Of those who won't be governed by their wives,/ Those old and angry, grudging all expense,/ God send them soon indeed the pestilence! (v. 36)

The Wife of Bath is a triumph of characterisation and represents Chaucer's true maturity of understanding the world in which he lives, as well as his true mastery of the poetic and creative art. Like the knight of the Wife's tale, Chaucer is a penitent seeking to leave behind and atone for the arrogant, misogynist and rapine attitude of his youth; he is first trying to be a better man and then a better human being. In the process, he acknowledges that the fault exists in himself (the male) rather than the unfortunate object of his attentions (the female). Nor does he pretend he is the victim of Satan's irresistible temptation or insidious suggestion, for the 'fiend' or 'devil' is only present in the Wife's tale as a casual curse or in the 'chide' of a male character's speech. Indeed, far from being punished as a victim or sinner, the knight is ultimately forgiven and rewarded with true love and the perfect wife at the end of his quest, when he allows the old woman to have 'sovereignty' over him. Thus, the last thing that the Wife can be is any creature of Satan. The male is the sinner who cannot control himself and needs a woman to rule him and keep him honest. Men are victims of themselves and no one else. Sin is its own punishment, and virtuous behaviour is its own reward. If Satan does exist, then he is just like us…

2.3 The familiar and the false friend

'The Wife of Bath's Tale' provides us with a new conception of Satan, one that is very different from the divine or punishing arbiter of the OT, the political persecutor of the NT, or the brutal appetites of the St George narrative. The Satan of *The Canterbury Tales* is just like us: familiar, friendly, engaging, urbane, humorous, earthy, domestic, casual, trivial, incidental, often banal and entirely satirical.

His most extended appearance is as a 'yeoman' in 'The Friar's Tale', when he provides such a mirror image to a travelling summoner that they become enamoured of each other as 'brothers sworn till their dying day, And r[i] de chatting pleasantly on their way' (v. 10). They tell each other everything, the summoner describing (or unwittingly confessing) his tricks, faithlessness, and sin in detail, and Satan describing his own particular nature, a nature that does not bother the summoner in the slightest. They both complain 'My lord is hard to me' and that 'My wages are scanty, right small ale' (v. 13). They resolve to help each other increase what they win by way of extortion, the summoner even seeking to show Satan new tricks. Finally, of course, it is in showing Satan the most wicked of extortions that the summoner sees his erstwhile victim damn him to hell (v. 41):

'Now, brother,' quoth the devil, 'be not wrath:/ Your body and this pan are mine by right./ You yet shall go to Hell with me tonight,/ Where you shall know of our mysteries/ More than does any master of divinity.'/ And with that the foul fiend dragged him hence;/ Body and soul he with devil went/ Where summoners receive their heritage.

A key aspect of this new conception of Satan is a shift towards the lower classes of society: where Christ is 'your champion and knight' (v. 41), Satan and the summoner are mere yeomen. Similarly, the high level political environment of Pergamon in the NT, where gods, emperors, kings and temple elders competed, and where Satan has his 'throne', is replaced in 'The Pardoner's Tale' with familiar characters and locations at the other end of the social spectrum: 'In Flanders once there was a company/ Of younger folk given all to folly,/ Such as riot, gambling, brothels, taverns,/ Where to the harps and lutes, and to citherns,/ They danced, and played at dice both day and night,/ And ate and drank more than wise men might,/ Offering thereby the devil sacrifice/ Within that devil's temple of cursed vice' (v. 1). Chaucer does not make this shift in order to sneer at the working classes particularly, but in order to make the concept of sin far less abstract or removed from our day-to-day lives and to help us recognise the dangers all around us. Satan, thereby, is far more identifiable, more easily recognised and even more *relatable*. If we do not remain vigilant, we can be drawn into sin as easily as we might turn to talk companionably to the person whom we are sat elbow-to-elbow with while drinking in a tavern. Clearly, this depiction of Satan sees him as more immediate, satirical, charming and subversive than previous incarnations, and perhaps therefore as even more terrifying. His *behaviour* is apparently more civilized, but Chaucer makes sure to remind us that his *nature* is as fundamentally base and grotesque as it ever was.

In the companion piece to 'The Friar's Tale', which is 'The Summoner's Prologue and Tale', we are presented with a Dantesque 'vision' of Satan in hell with a bestial 'tail' and a 'nest' of friars 'swarming' in and from his 'arse' (v. 1). Satan is silent in the vision, raises his tail upon command and otherwise 'lay[s] still' (v. 1). It seems, then, that Satan only speaks to us in our own words (after all, he is denied and denies 'the word of God') and only becomes animated by way of the opportunity of our own self-regarding intent and desire (v. 1):

To his body again […] he awoke./ But nevertheless for fear still he shook,/ The devil's arse was there yet in his mind;/ Such is the heritage of all his kind.

Combined with this shift towards the lower classes to increase Satan's mass appeal and social relevance, then, there is a shift towards and yet further increase in Satan's physicality and actuality. There is a scatological – and arguably homoerotic – obsession with his reality/realness which is reflected in the summoner's extended discussion with Satan concerning the devil's physical and metaphysical nature, 'element' and composition. Satan, therefore, is very much self-actualised by and within English culture and cultural identity, within the famous English appetite for – and the nature of its particular styles of – subversive humour, within its entertaining social irreverence, its vain individualism, and its creative and artistic self-expression. This is very much a summary of what *The Canterbury Tales* as a complete work states, enacts, reflects and represents for us, the readers and audience. We see that we are our own worst enemy, even when we like to insist that it is the foreigner or outsider who brings evil amongst us – be it the 'dark' Muslims of the St George narrative in 'The Man of Law's Tale', the Flemish Satan-worshippers at the start of 'The Pardoner's Tale', the Jews who give an ear to Satan in 'The Prioress's Tale', or the inhabitants of a corrupt Rome in 'The General Prologue'. After all, *The Canterbury Tales* exposes the flaws within a group of people from all parts and all walks of life of English society, ironically people who pridefully believe they are on a religious pilgrimage and journey towards salvation and spiritual advancement:

'Ah,' quoth the summoner, 'benedicite!/ What's this? I thought you were a yeoman, truly;/ You have a man's shape as well as me./ Have you another shape determinate/ In Hell, where you are in your own true state?/ 'Nay, for sure,' quoth he, 'there have we none./ But when we choose,

then we can don one,/ Or else make you believe we have
a shape./ Sometimes we're like a man, or like an ape,/ Or
like an angel can I ride and go./ It is no wondrous thing
though it be so;/ A louse-ridden juggler can deceive thee,/
And, pardee, I've much more power than he.'/ 'Why,'
quoth the summoner, 'do you ride and run/ In sundry
shape, and not always in one?'/ 'That we,' quoth he, 'may
such forms awake/ As are most useful when our prey we
take.'/ […]'Then tell me,' quoth the summoner, 'speak
no lie,/ Make you your new bodies thus always/ From the
elements?' The fiend answered: 'Nay./ Sometimes we're
illusions, sometimes rise/ With corpses' bodies in sundry
wise,/ And speak as fluently and fair and well/ As, to the
Witch of Endor, Samuel./ (And yet some men say it was
not he –/ I grant no worth to your theology.)/ But one thing
I warn you of, it's no jape:/ You'll know one day how we
find a shape;/ You shall hereafter, my brother dear,/ Come
where you need not lend an ear!/ For you will, from your
own experience,/ Be able to lecture in word and sentence/
Better than Virgil when he was alive,/ Or Dante.
('The Friar's Tale', v. 17-21)

As we also see from the above, in Chaucer's work and in
Chaucer's time the supernatural was considered entirely real.
Satan literally walked – in disguise – amongst the British, in
Britain. He had necromantic power to raise the dead and use
their bodies as zombie-like vehicles for his will. He also had
witches (in the vein of the Witch of Endor) to serve his will
and to raise, question and torture the spirits of the dead. He
had magic and wilfulness that competed for 'sovereignty'
with our own selfish free will, vain wilfulness and defiant
independence. For Chaucer, it was only through the sacrifice
of that defiant independence, through self-sacrifice, by

putting an end to selfishness and to obsessive self-interest and by recognising the virtue of God's 'sovereignty' over us that Satan could be left impotent, immobile and ineffectual. Anything else meant 'doing a deal with the devil' of the type that we see in 'The Friar's Tale', or using our free will to consent to Satan having sovereignty over us. It is a trope that becomes fully developed once we get to Christopher Marlowe's play of *Doctor Faustus* (c.1588-93), written at a time when England had recently split from Rome (via 1534's Act of Supremacy) and set up an independent Church. Doctor John Dee, the inspiration for Marlowe's main character, was a necromancer and magician to Queen Elizabeth I's court, when witches were believed to be at large and the Witchcraft Act had just been passed (1563). In those years, England was fighting Spain to protect English sovereignty and independence (1588) and it was beginning to establish an empire for itself. Also, during this period the English language, its creative expression and a new sense of cultural identity were being born. It was both a literal and metaphorical 'renaissance', a renaissance that required yet another shift in its conception of Satan if this figure and the evil it represented were to remain relevant and recognisable.

The Renaissance saw Europe making massive strides in its knowledge and mapping of the world (with Columbus's 'discovery of the New World in 1492'), its scientific understanding of the universe (with, for example, Nicolaus Copernicus placing the Sun at the centre rather than the Earth and Galileo Gallilei making advances in physics, applied mathematics and astronomy) and how it discovered, captured and disseminated new knowledge (with Galileo's 'scientific method', Luca Pacioli's work in book-keeping and accounting and of course Gutenberg's printing press), which in turn inspired – if not required – advances in religious thinking, the philosophical sciences, art, music and literature.

Fundamentally, the Renaissance saw Europe arriving at a new understanding and appreciation of what it was to be human (the latter also helped by Leonardo da Vinci's and Andreas Vesalius's work on anatomy and the mechanics of biology). Thereby, the Renaissance saw humanity able to take a more proactive control of the world around us, rather than simply continuing to react to and endure greater and possibly divine forces, meaning humanity was now empowered and powerfully different. This, then, was the *Humanism* or *Essentialism* of the Renaissance: humankind was in and of itself powerful, valuable, self-sufficient, self-improving and to be gloriously celebrated, rather than exclusively meaningful as a part of God's creation, in serving God or as judged by God. Here, too, was the new temptation and possibility of evil: humankind could look inward for salvation or becoming self-regarding rather than only look outward or upward for God's mercy.

The temptation put before the Renaissance individual, particularly one who had become a master of the sciences and was still hungry to learn more, was that they turn their entire attention (from God) towards winning near-divine knowledge and power over the world. The temptation for the doctor of sciences was to seek to replace God Himself. This precisely describes the Satanic temptation, plot and ultimate damnation of Doctor Faustus. In the play, through natural intelligence and scholarship, Faustus has become a Doctor at the University of Wittenberg. Having mastered 'logic', medicine, law and theology, and still wanting to learn more, he turns to learning necromancy and magic, pursuits that promise to provide him the divine power of resurrection, the 'forbidden knowledge' that grants power over all in Creation and immortality. In the prologue of the play, we have the foreshadowing of Faustus being likened to Icarus, who fatally flies too close to the sun with manmade and unnatural science and technology. We may also be reminded of Eden's 'forbidden fruit' of knowledge. Yet it is really this play which first furnishes us with the motif of 'the over-reaching scientist', a motif which later occurs throughout the English literature of Britain's Industrial Revolution era (described in the next chapter).

During the Renaissance, this age of Humanism and Essentialism, the Satanic is very much within us as a part of us (rather than any sort of external, malign force), an aspect of our own intellectual, physical and *psychological* capacity, appetite and drive. The play *Doctor Faustus* is very much a physical enactment of the intellectual and psychological debate, development and doom going on within Faustus's own mind. Although the audience sees physical representations of the Good Angel, the Bad Angel, Lucifer and various other demons during the early scenes of Faustus's mental deliberation, these characters are entirely invisible to him. Therefore, Faustus's thoughts, mental/psychological space and relative state of grace are directly mapped onto the physical characters, physical space and actual plot development of the play. The real and spiritual, the physical and metaphysical and the religious and scientific are one and the same. It is this all-encompassing 'conceit' which gives *Doctor Faustus* such extraordinary power. It is this conceit that famously caused such panic and 'madness' when Renaissance audiences came to believe that an 'extra' and actual demon had appeared on the stage before them, conjured by the play's profanity (Prynne, 1632). When asked how Mephistopholes is out of hell, the demon replies (p. 15):

Why this is hell, nor am I out of it./ Think'st thou that I, who saw the face of God,/ And tasted the eternal joys of heaven,/ Am not tormented with ten thousand hells/ In being deprived of everlasting bliss?

Having pursued knowledge of necromancy (via a human magician and witchcrafter), Faustus uses it to conjure Mephistopholes (who is also Lucifer) in the hope of learning the magic that will allow him power over the world. Mephistopholes agrees to serve Faustus magically for 24 years in return for Faustus's soul. Faustus cuts his arm in order to sign the contract in his own blood, when the wound is divinely healed and the warning words of *Homo, fuge!* (Man, flee!) appear on his skin. Considering himself already damned, and therefore with nowhere to flee, Faustus chooses to act further against his own being by using coals brought by Mephistopholes to reopen the wound and then use his blood to seal his own final damnation.

Faustus is encouraged and served by Mephistopholes throughout, but the decisions are Faustus's alone. It is his selfish desire and will that wins him magic with divine potential. However, because his will operates based on (or is corrupted by) selfishness, instead of performing miracles to help others, Faustus's magic merely provides diverting entertainment or constant vexation for others. He becomes famous for his powers, but always needs an audience and, in the end, does nothing worthwhile. With all the wealth in the world, and even with Helen of Troy as his lover (a silent and long-dead ghost), Faustus's life is meaningless, empty and literally soulless. His only constant companion is Mephistopholes, but this familiar is only ever trivial, roundabout, clownish, pedantic or tiresome. Mephistopholes is 'familiar' and occasionally sympathetic, but no true friend, and at the eleventh hour he finally drags Faustus off to hell.

Having started 'base of stock', as the prologue to the play tells us, Faustus is literally a self-made man. Through a combination of intellect and tireless hard work, he elevates himself socially and is the quintessential Renaissance man. His determination, self-improvement, independence of thought and consideration of the human condition mean he is initially admired and identified with, by the audience. Yet it is his insistence upon being self-made (rejecting his original Maker and thereby refusing the possibility of genuine repentance) which sees him doomed to damnation. Faustus is a 'tragical' figure (following the Aristotelean model and the full title of the 1620 printing of the play), therefore, one for whom we have a certain sympathy. There, but for the grace of God, go we. For the Renaissance audience, Faustus's ending would have been as real and shocking as it was a salutary lesson.

Yet what is that lesson precisely? It has been the subject of heated debate since the time of the play's original performances and Prynne's Puritan polemic *Histriomastix* of 1632. If every Renaissance individual were to pursue self-improvement through independence of thought and pushing at the limits of knowledge, would that see England thrown into 'misrule' and disorder, then dragged to hell? Would the soul of England be lost to Satan? Was Marlowe criticising England's independence from Rome (and at the time there was speculation he was Catholic)? Surely not, for in the play the Pope and the Pope's court are made to look self-important and decadent fools by Mephistopholes. The lesson or message then is more complex and – like the play – more of a description of current thinking concerning the wider human condition rather than any prescription of 'correct' social behaviours. All but tautologously, that description is enacted in the play via the particular characterisations and unique relationship of Faustus and his demonic familiar, who is as familiar as our own selves, a Satan who is an aspect of our own essential nature and original sin. Satan is, at last, no longer an *external* agency who seeks to victimise us or act upon the agency of our free will; he is now *internal* to us and an essential aspect of us. If he acts in the wider world, then he is but a physical manifestation of our selfish, vain and proud free will. He is a psychological aspect of ourselves; he is, if you will allow it, the dark id to our bright ego.

From the above, Marlowe's Lucifer very much represents a mindset or philosophical position for the Renaissance individual (Faustus) that becomes its own doom or self-fulfilling prophecy. A corollary of this is that in the play Faustus's sin is not any sort of selfish *action* taken against humankind; rather, it is just the intellectual, metaphysical and philosophical decision not to be content with the physical and social limitations of his birth and creation by God. Implicitly, this decision is a rejection of God based upon personal ambition for self-empowerment and self-improvement. It embraces the 'magic' and power of free will as that which allows us to self-actualise. It is also a warning, however, that when that power is not used in the service of our fellow man then it is self-indulgent, vain, self-corrupting and implicitly self-harming. When the virtuous (and therefore generous) individual uses free will as the magic or agency of their desire then miracles are their reward, but when the sinfully selfish individual uses free will as the magic or agency of their desire then they betray and damn themselves.

Marlowe's play is a step towards understanding Satan as a particular human character or set of characteristics of which the majority of us are capable. It is a character which most of us can identify with, if not admire, and it is a character who becomes fully manifest in Milton's *Paradise Lost* (1672 and 1674). In this epic poem concerning the creation and nature of Man, the glorious protagonist of the early books (chapters) is Satan. He is highly intelligent, sophisticated of thought, independent, self-made ('self-begot', 'self-raised', book 5), given to rhetorically powerful speeches, a charismatic and natural leader of his kind, a skilled politician, a fearless warrior and a revolutionary who resists a tyrant (God). We first meet this Satan in book 1 suffering in a lake of fire in hell. We cannot help but feel a certain 'sympathy' for this magnificent, defeated being, particularly as his is the narrative perspective. That sympathy only increases when Satan, having organised and bolstered his broken followers, volunteers to undertake the challenging task of corrupting the newly created and now most divinely favoured Earth. In order to get to Earth, Satan has to brave the dangers of the Abyss alone, as if he is on some Greek heroic quest, where the difficulties that are overcome are as much a test of fortitude of character as they are of anything else. It is not going too far to say that this Satan is so sympathetic, persuasive and characterful that he is likeable.

As the poem unfolds, however, we see more and more just how self-serving Satan is, and that this is his self-defeating flaw. We also come to understand that the rebellion he led in heaven was not because of the tyranny of God but because he wanted to see his own wants served rather than God's. There is now something about Satan of the peevish and unruly child rebelling against their parent. There is something of the jealous sibling in how Satan sets out to spoil things for Adam, so that Adam will no longer be the favourite. *Paradise Lost*, then, tells the story of the Fall in tragic terms, where our own strength of character and determination are also our weakness. Behaving with a strength of virtue and self-sacrifice (like Christ) sees us closer to God, but acting selfishly to weaken others sees us taken so far from God that we only make a hell of our own lives.

> The mind is its own place, and in itself
> Can make a Heaven of Hell, a Hell of Heaven (Hughes,
> book 1, l. 254-55)

When acting based solely on our ego, we are made in Satan's own image rather than God's. We are driven by selfish wants and act with a bestial aggression to see them fulfilled, placing them ahead of any social or moral concern. Hence, through the course of the poem, the once magnificent and kingly Satan degenerates physically, taking the form of a lesser angel (cherub), then a ravening cormorant in the Tree of Life, then an earth-bound lion and tiger, and finally a toad and a snake. Our own friends no longer recognise us, for none of the angels initially know the changed Satan in book 5, and when he returns to his throne in hell he looks like nothing more than a self-indulgent, drunken debauchee (of the tragicomic Falstaffian type).

Here, too, is the image of the fallen and degenerate King. It was during Milton's own lifetime that Charles I was executed (1649), a King who was notoriously vain, self-indulgent and unrepentant. The Satan of *Paradise Lost* is every inch such a king, one who inevitably damns himself. It is civil society and a Puritan self-discipline that win out during Milton's time and serve as such a contrast to the Satanic character and renaissance potential of humankind. Let us not forget that Satan is also initially cast as a revolutionary in *Paradise Lost* but, like the autocratic Cromwell of his later years, this is a revolutionary more interested in self-elevation than the wider good, and so a revolutionary who will also bring about his own fall. Our fight against Satan, therefore, is a fight against ourselves, and one way perhaps of describing the Second English Civil War. It is only through self-discipline, recognising a law above us, keeping certain checks upon our free will, and not hesitating to act in the interests of wider society that we prevent ourselves from being and acting as Satan himself and turning our world into a hell. It asks a great deal of an individual, to be sure, but it was taken entirely seriously by the Puritans, to the extent that they frowned upon humour generally. An act of Parliament in 1644 even banned dancing, plays, games, singing carols, frivolity and drinking at Christmas, effectively banning Christmas as a festival. Their souls were at stake, after all.

England was now saved from the wanton excesses of the Renaissance and Satan was now expelled from our shores and minds. The country was united under God and its own Church, and now the centre of a growing Christian empire on earth. That 'first British empire' was to grow and thrive for another hundred years, until the American Revolution of 1783. Then the British were to look for even greater technologies with which to master their environment, enemies and lives. They were to enter the Great Industrial Revolution, a time that offered them terrible infernal engines and dark Satanic mills. What on earth could go wrong when they had such tools and weapons at their command?

3. The science of Satan

As shown in the previous chapter, Satan managed to thrive amongst humankind for thousands of years by a being a master of shape-shifting, assuming the form in each era or period of history that kept him most socially relevant and an everyday part of our lives. He even managed to convince us that he was an essential aspect of our own hearts and minds, so that we would turn against ourselves, flagellating, testing and punishing each other, visiting misery, confinement and torture upon each other, and actually doing his job for him. We even went as far as killing each other and saying we killed *in God's own name*! By so doing, we sinned against ourselves and damned ourselves. Not only had we committed the ultimate sin and blasphemy, but it also saw even enlightened thinkers begin to turn away from God's own church – after all, who would want any part of a church that would sanction the slaughter or enslavement of thousands or millions of innocents (be it the people of the Middle East during the Crusades or the people of Africa during the colonial period)?

As we will see in this chapter, writers of the nineteenth century therefore began to turn away from God and divine will as the logocentre, the organising function, the driving aspect of plot (impetus) or the resolution of their narratives. Instead, they applied themselves to a closer consideration and study of the human body and mind, human agency and socio-political responsibility and consequence (social justice, democracy and common law rather than divine dictate, Divine Right and class privilege). That is to say, they embraced scientific theory and tools in orders to better understand humankind, the human condition and the possibility of existential answers.

The risk for Satan, naturally, in humankind's move away from religion towards science was that he would be perceived more and more as a superstition and anachronism, and less and less as an essential aspect of ourselves. The risk, for Satan, was that science (and the philosophies of science fiction) would liberate humankind and see them transcend their lesser (sinful) selves. Satan would be reduced to a historical footnote, he would no longer live (remain animated) through us and he would effectively cease to exist.

The literature of the nineteenth century onwards thus became the story of Satan's fight for survival. His ambition (literary and literal), as first witnessed in Milton's *Paradise Lost*, was to have himself as the hero of the piece, a hero who successfully completes his quest and secures total victory. His ambition was to shift his representation from that anti-hero who ultimately fails in Paradise Lost to the roguish and charming hero who is ultimately enthroned, even if a good number of other leading characters have to suffer and fall along the way.

Could he possibly succeed? As Brandon Sanderson asked on the UK cover of *The Final Empire* (2009), 'What if the dark lord won?'. What if Daenerys Targaryen in *Game of Thrones* (2011) finally brought her Dothraki horde and dragons across the sea and laid waste to Westeros during the sort of reign of 'fire and blood' (the words of House Targaryen) not seen since the time of the last 'mad' Targaryen monarch, Aerys II? What if the superhuman and supra-intelligent Khan (played by Benedict Cumberbatch) of *Star Trek: Into Darkness* (2013) did manage to bring his followers out of their frozen state, wrest control of the mighty ship Vengeance and take down the Federation? What if we had misunderstood the nature of God and He was already dead, as in Philip Pullman's *His Dark Materials* (1995-2000)? What if we were to discover we were simply the late Cylon creations of ancient Capricans, as per *Battlestar Galactica* (2004-08), or the most advanced creations of the *Westworld* (2016 onwards) theme park? In the move away from God towards science, and with Dracula and Lucifer finally securing the lead roles in their own TV shows (2014 and 2016 respectively), wouldn't Satan be our new hero, role model and idol? Would he not guide us, inspire us and be nominated our champion, leader, president and more? What if he were worshipped by audiences, the media and entire nations?

What if? If Satan were to become the hero, what would humanity be reduced to? The role of the anti-hero who ultimately fails? Or something somehow *less* than human? What if? What then, puny human?

3.1 The scientist and the monster

The new possibilities and horrific consequences presented to the individual and to society at large when turning away from God as organising function were first explored in novel form by Horace Walpole's hugely successful *The Castle of Otranto* (1764). Sub-titled 'A Gothic Story' and the first novel to claim such label for itself, *The Castle of Otranto* is indeed 'generally considered to be the first Gothic novel' (Groom, 2014). It is full of portentous dreams, the animated dead, bloody visions, secret passageways, the surreal and romance. It tells the story of Manfred, the lord of the castle of Otranto, whose son (Conrad) dies on his wedding day when a six-foot helmet crushes him. Ignoring the ominous nature of the death and a prophecy that his family will lose the lordship, Manfred resolves to give over his own wife so that he might have the young bride-to-be (Isabella) for himself and thereby secure the family line. Unwilling as she is, Isabella flees the now monstrous and cruel Manfred. Manfred's determination and appetites apparently end up undoing the natural order of things (bringing disorder to the inner mind and its experience of the external world), his family, relations with the neighbouring kingdom and his own lordship. Like Satan in *Paradise Lost*, then, Manfred is the anti-hero who drives the plot forward, sacrificing whatever is necessary, but eventually failing. Therefore, although Satan has now been replaced in the narrative by an entirely human character, and although there is an attempt to turn away from traditional religious strictures, the narrative stubbornly remains within a religious framework of symbolism, judgement and moral lesson. In this sense, *The Castle of Otranto*, for all that it is the first Gothic novel, with a new or 'novel' style (mixing the ancient and modern styles of romance, with resulting discordant moments and horror elements) and containing 'novelty' (as described in Walpole's preface to the second edition), does not fully manage to transgress or step beyond the limits of a traditional allegory or morality play. What it does do, however, is offer a step in the 'right direction', a brief lifting of the veil, a glimpse of the forbidden, a new creative potential and elusive promise of, if not transcendence then transition to, an altered state and future.

For all its potential and for all its suggestion that through force of will Man might be able to transcend the lowly position of his birth or the limitations of his place in the world, *The Castle of Otranto* ultimately asserts the natural and moral order of God's creation. Manfred is punished for his over-reaching ambition when, in a moment of mistaken identity, he murders his own daughter. Seeing the horror of what he has done, he repents and vows to lead a good and religious life with his wife from that day onwards. There is also a moment of *deus ex machina* when the ghost of the martyred but rightful heir to the castle of Otranto (Prince Alfonso) appears and declares Theodore's right of succession. Theodore marries Isabella, the princess of the neighbouring kingdom, takes over the rulership of Otranto and brings peace to all. The tropes of romance and a Shakespearean comedy thereby win out over the Satanic tropes of horror.

Somewhat anticlimactically, *The Castle of Otranto* ends up as a melodramatic celebration of Divine Right, the right of succession and the rule of the upper classes. Even the domestic affairs of the upper classes are seen to have more value, significance and consequence than the concerns of ordinary people, since Manfred's actions and moral state are directly reflected in nature and the wider environment, a nature and environment that affect all others. Also, the way that the story ends for Manfred makes it clear that even the selfish desires and wilfulness of the upper classes are more elevated, nuanced and permissible than they are for others: although he loses the rulership, this has only really gone to the right person; although Manfred has behaved in a monstrous and rapine manner, the repentant ending allows that his behaviour was necessarily driven by his *droit du seigneur* (the right of the lord to take all other men's wives on the wedding day) and the requirement to secure an heir; although his intent is to murder Isabella at one point, the fact that he kills his own daughter means his own fatherhood and 'property' have now suffered such loss that he needs no further punishment; hence, Manfred's 'nobility' and state of grace based on his 'rightful' position are secure and properly evident when all is settled.

In summary, although the new possibilities and horrific consequences offered when there is a turning away from God as the organising function (of our lives and any narrative) are explored in part by *The Castle of Otranto*, they are never fully resolved in creative, artistic or philosophical terms. The 'new possibilities' are sentimentally excessive, sexually extreme, perverse, not worth pursuing or just plain silliness, while the 'horrific consequences' are all too often confusing, random, surreal, laughably unrealistic or simply too overblown and exaggerated in physical size and apparent significance.

It is not until Mary Shelley's novel *Frankenstein or, The Modern Prometheus* (1818) that the new possibilities and horrific consequences are given a more serious and extended consideration. *The Castle of Otranto* was the first Gothic novel, but it was backward-looking in its romantic use of medieval knights and pastoral motifs and its construction of a plot based on Renaissance comedy and revenge tragedy tropes, not to mention the grounding of the text in the preface as a 1529 account of events which 'must have been between 1095, the era of the first crusade, and 1243'. *Frankenstein*, on the other hand, was the first 'modern' novel (as per the novel's sub-title) and far more forward-looking in its consideration of scientific and social development. Where *The Castle of Otranto*, like many works before it, concerned itself with the wherebys, wherefores, and the relative state of grace of the self-obsessed upper classes, *Frankenstein* concerned itself with a middle-class scientist who suffers the death of his mother early in life and sets out to discover the secrets of life so that all might achieve that happier life or state of grace that exists when we no longer have to suffer grief:

I need not describe the feelings of those whose dearest ties
are rent by that most irreparable evil, the void that presents
itself to the soul, and the despair that is exhibited on the
countenance. It is so long before the mind can persuade
itself that she whom we saw every day and whose very
existence appeared a part of our own can have departed
forever – that the brightness of a beloved eye can have been
extinguished and the sound of a voice so familiar and dear
to the ear can be hushed, never more to be heard. These
are the reflections of the first days; but when the lapse of
time proves the reality of the evil, then the actual bitterness
of grief commences. Yet from whom has not that rude
hand rent away some dear connection? And why should I
describe a sorrow which all have felt, and must feel?
(Shelley, p. 43)

We should wonder what occurred in Britain's socio-
history between the publication of *The Castle of Otranto*
(1764) and *Frankenstein* (1818) to see such a significant shift
in narrative approach: from a plot progression relying on
divine warning, judgement and intervention, to a plot driven
by human decision, discovery and (mis)judgement; from
the selfish and indulged upper classes, to the self-aware and
self-sacrificing middle and working classes; from essential
but irrational passions, to a restless but rational pursuit of
learning and progress; from a subjective understanding
of and response to the world around us, to an empirical
measurement and scientific harnessing of natural forces. Put
simply, the Industrial Revolution had begun, a time that saw
science and technology 'freeing' the masses from a lifetime
of purely physical labour, that saw them having more time
and money for education and entertainment, that saw them
socially advancing, that saw them better able to resist

traditional social conditioning and the ways of thinking proscribed by such human institutions as human churches, the class system and patriarchy.

It was in such a socio-historical context that the female author Mary Shelley produced the sympathetic narrative of *Frankenstein*. It was in such a context that we are given a shockingly brave narrative that replaces God as our maker with a human scientist as the creator of life. As per the 'Author's Introduction' to the novel, Mary Shelley was inspired and emboldened to write the novel in 1816 while staying in Switzerland with her poet husband Percy Shelley close by the Villa Diodati, which was being rented by Lord Byron and his physician John Polidori. The sojourn at the Villa Diodati is a notorious moment, celebrated in popular culture and anecdotally used to refer to the origins and emergence of the gothic and horror genres, and to illustrate how some of the greatest expressions of 'the Romantic imagination' came about[1]. The sojourn also, in microcosm, represented the socio-historical context previously mentioned. During an electrical storm over the villa's lake, or so the story goes, Byron read German ghost stories[2] aloud (perhaps with a magic lantern, smoke and ventriloquism) to scare his guests, and then challenged them to write their own stories. Also fuelling their imaginations would have been laudanum liberally supplied by Polidori, the sexually charged atmosphere created by Claire Clairmont's presence (society had been scandalised by this young lower middle-class woman's out-of-wedlock affair with Byron) and the fact that Mary may previously have had her own flirtation with Byron, and the intellectual friction and frisson coming from animated discussions concerning Romantic philosophy, religion (Percy Shelley was a well-known atheist), heurism,

1. As flamboyantly enacted in Ken Russell's movie Gothic (1986)
2. From the *Fantasmagoriana* (1812)

galvanism, social change (Mary and Claire's father had been an ardent anarchist), the nature of Man and transcendence (BBC, 2016). In short, the novel of *Frankenstein* was the feverish and inspired creation of Mary Shelley and the context in which she was living, just as the 'monster' was the feverish and inspired creation of Doctor Frankenstein. Indeed, the all-important 'moment of creation' enacted by Frankenstein in the novel shares signature features with the time and place of the novel's writing (as detailed by Mary in the Author's Introduction): from the electrical storm, to the flickering candlelight, the night-terrors, the visions of a 'hideous phantasm' and 'a ghostly image', 'some powerful engine' and 'the stupendous mechanism of the Creator of the world'. Therefore, in terms of its *initial* spark, conception and impetus, *Frankenstein* represents an ecstatic vision of the glory and power that human ingenuity and daring (the Romantic imagination) combined with the tools of learning, discovery and invention (the science and technology of the Industrial Revolution) can achieve: the true ascension of Man; the attainment of an eternal state of grace and transcendence; immortality and godhead. The following quotation appears on the title page of the 1818 first edition, quoting Satan himself and rejecting the primacy of God's ability to create:

> Did I request thee, Maker, from my clay
> To mould me Man, did I solicit thee
> From darkness to promote me?
> (Paradise Lost, X, 743-45)

At the same time, of course, Frankenstein is also a nightmarish vision of the absolute damnation and horror that human over-reaching (for the forbidden fruit of knowledge) and fallibility can visit upon us. After all, the 'moment of creation' first sees nature torn asunder by a storm and then, via the actions of the monster, the fundamental order and integrity of Doctor Frankenstein's familial and social relationships undone (the alienation and death of all of the Doctor's immediate family, local villagers he encounters, his bride-to-be and his lifelong friend Henry)... until he himself succumbs, alone in the middle of a frozen and desolate wasteland. However, it is in its consideration of the true nature of evil (or the Satanic) that the novel is also somewhat ambivalent. Although Doctor Frankenstein's act of creation verges on the monstrously blasphemous, and although he creates a 'monster', neither Doctor Frankenstein's original intention nor the monster's original nature are actually evil. On the part of the creature, this is evident in his claim: 'I am thy creature: I ought to be thy Adam, but I am rather the fallen angel, whom thou drivest from joy for no misdeed' (p. 95). Doctor Frankenstein, on his part, is no less appalled by his own doing when he realises what he has created:

> I collected the instruments of life around me, that I might infuse a spark of being into the lifeless thing that lay at my feet. It was already one in the morning; the rain pattered dismally against the panes, and my candle was nearly burnt out, when, by the glimmer of the half-extinguished light, I saw the dull yellow eye of the creature open; it breathed hard, and a convulsive motion agitated its limbs.
> How can I describe my emotions at this catastrophe, or how delineate the wretch whom with such infinite pains and care I had endeavoured to form? His limbs were in proportion, and I had selected his features as beautiful. Beautiful! - Great God! His yellow skin scarcely covered the work

of muscles and arteries beneath; his hair was of a lustrous black, and flowing; his teeth of a pearly whiteness; but these luxuriances only formed a more horrid contrast with his watery eyes, that seemed almost of the same colour as the dun white sockets in which they were set, his shrivelled complexion and straight black lips.
(Shelley, p. 56)

Principally, in the novel, evil is of our own making. Evil is of ourselves. It is as familiar as our own reflection, and yet it is not our entire selves or our better selves. It means we do not entirely recognise ourselves in the mirror. There is something fascinatingly 'wrong' about us. Is it even human? What is it to be human then? What does all our observation, measurement, science and technology tell us? What do our instincts tell us? What do the hairs rising on the back of our necks tell us? Are we secretly thrilled by it? Are we entirely terrified and appalled? Are we undone by it just as Doctor Frankenstein is constantly swooning, falling ill, having feverish dreams, falling back overwhelmed or otherwise being paralysed in the novel?

We do not entirely recognise ourselves, but beauty still remains in the eye of the beholder. It is only once Frankenstein *rejects* his creation that the evil acts in the novel actually begin. The act of creation itself is not the evil: it is our fear of and our subsequent refusal to embrace difference, our own occasional lack of courage, curiosity and ambition, our lack of sympathy and our cruel judgement of others. The society we create is not in and of itself evil, but when that society starts to insist upon what is (not) 'allowed' then it is perpetrating an evil by exiling that which is different.

There is a grand irony in that, just as the novel describes the grand irony of Frankenstein seeking to create life but only succeeding in causing so much death. It would be tempting to see the device of the grand irony as the universe or the divine passing some sort of judgement upon Frankenstein for his blasphemous transgression, but there is no divine intervention in this novel: all the deaths that occur are as a direct consequence of the actions and emotional responses of the scientist and his monster. Therefore, finally we enact judgement upon ourselves. And we cannot escape ourselves. The scientist creates and seals his own fate. With his maker dead, the monster is left utterly alone in the world, devastated and shunned, without solace or comfort. Empty and without meaning – a personification of the grief and evil 'void' of the mother's death.

"Farewell! I leave you, and in you the last of humankind whom these eyes will ever behold. Farewell, Frankenstein! If thou wert yet alive and yet cherished a desire of revenge against me, it would be better satiated in my life than in my destruction. But it was not so; thou didst seek my extinction, that I might not cause greater wretchedness; and if yet, in some mode unknown to me, thou hadst not ceased to think and feel, thou wouldst not desire against me a vengeance greater than that which I feel. Blasted as thou wert, my agony was still superior to thine, for the bitter sting of remorse will not cease to rankle in my wounds until death shall close them forever.
"But soon," he cried with sad and solemn enthusiasm, "I shall die, and what I now feel be no longer felt. Soon these burning miseries will be extinct. I shall ascend my funeral pile triumphantly and exult in the agony of the torturing flames. The light of that conflagration will fade away; my ashes will be swept into the sea by the winds. My spirit will sleep in peace, or if it thinks, it will not surely think thus. Farewell."
(Shelley, p. 211)

In gifting us free will and true independence, the Maker is very much absent in essential respects. We exist in the tragedy of that circumstance and the world feels a cold, uncaring, bleak (Godforsaken) and *abortive* place: we exist as the tragedy. If the Maker is watching us from hiding, just as the reader watches the scientist and monster play out their lives, he or she might well be moved to quiet tears. Or the Maker is indeed dead.

Where lies hope then? Hope lie in the *what if?* What if Doctor Frankenstein had embraced his creation and nurtured it, so that it could have become a true angel existing in a state of grace? What if the scientist had gifted the monster a bride, instead of dismembering that female body? What if the monster changed his mind and decided not to immolate himself? Would the monster discover some sort of immortality (his dead flesh, by the power of galvanism, always animated afresh) and some manner of contentment? Would the monster learn to gift life to its own creations and evolve an entire race of monsters? Would the monster then be the Maker? Would the monster embrace its own creations or reject them? And so the story repeats and cycles. For it is the eternal story, that same story of God rejecting Satan (or vice versa) that we considered in the first chapter.

From the above, we see then that we *are* Satan or Satanic. Our nature is fallen, flawed, originally sinful and ugly. Our potential is as angelic as it is demonic, however. That is not metaphorical or symbolic, but a statement of actuality.

Science, technology and knowledge are the tools by which we understand, recognise and animate our own potential. If we were to resist such tools, we would be ignorant (of even ourselves) but exist in some sort of blissful innocence (as per the Garden of Eden).

The novel *Frankenstein*, in the end, is ambivalent about whether we should entirely resist such tools, such Satanic instruments, infernal devices, 'powerful engine[s]' and 'the stupendous mechanism of the Creator'. Certainly, we should not over-reach with such tools, as Doctor Frankenstein discovers, and as the framing narrator Captain Walton comes to appreciate, giving up on his stubborn endeavour to find the mythical Northwest Passage[3], an endeavour which – it is implied – would only lead to his death. Yet how can they be resisted entirely when God has gifted us with imagination and the knowledge contained in the Bible, and when science has the potential to improve the lot of the common person? Put simply, just as Frankenstein yearns to discover, and just as the monster yearns for acknowledgement, companionship and definition (for without it there is no hope and only a despair like the 'void' of the mother's death), we cannot entirely resist such science, and God would not have it otherwise, for He has made the need essential to our beings.

In *Frankenstein*, then, we are a dual-self: a commixture of the angelic and demonic, of the scientist and monster, of enlightened intellect and destructive passion, and of self-sacrificing virtue and self-aggrandising sin. Only a proper understanding of that self allows us to guard against its negative potential and damnation. Only by using science to understand properly ourselves and our nature can we best guard against our worse nature. Only by understanding the horrors of the Satanic and the awful possibilities of power in the wrong hands can we prepare ourselves to defend against it.

---

3. The Northwest Passage was not discovered until 1850, so at the time of *Frankenstein* (1818) was still a foolhardy quest or like Captain Ahab's great white whale in *Moby-Dick* (1851).

3.2 The vampire and his reflection

Surely *Frankenstein*'s pairing of the scientist and monster anticipates and does something of the philosophical groundwork for the emergence of the 'science of the mind' and Freud's scientific identification of the dual-self in terms of ego and id, and his theories concerning the superego function and multiple personalities. Certainly, Robert Louise Stevenson's *The Strange Case of Dr Jekyll and Mr Hyde* owes much to *Frankenstein* in how it understands the scientist and the monster as dual aspects of the same mind. Gone are the days when a person's mental distraction, poor behaviour or extreme passions might all too easily be put down to 'demonic possession' and a certain victimhood: now, through an improved and medical understanding of both the individual and the functioning of the mind, humankind can potentially be responsible for itself and safeguard itself. Science, then, perhaps offers us the potential to imprison or 'cage' Satan. These are the themes that are enacted and described in Stevenson's tale:

[…]when I slept, or when the virtue of the medicine wore off, I would leap almost without transition (for the pangs of transformation grew daily less marked) into the possession of a fancy brimming with images of terror, a soul boiling with causeless hatreds, and a body that seemed not strong enough to contain the raging energies of life. The powers of Hyde seemed to have grown with the sickliness of Jekyll. And certainly the hate that now divided them was equal on each side. With Jekyll, it was a thing of vital instinct. He had now seen the full deformity of that creature that shared with him some of the phenomena of consciousness, and was co-heir with him to death: and beyond these links of community, which in themselves made the most poignant part of his distress, he thought of Hyde, for all his energy of life, as of something not only hellish but inorganic. This was the shocking thing; that the slime of the pit seemed to utter cries and voices; that the amorphous dust gesticulated and sinned; that what was dead, and had no shape, should usurp the offices of life. And this again, that that insurgent horror was knit to him closer than a wife, closer than an eye; lay caged in his flesh, where he heard it mutter and felt it struggle to be born

(Stevenson, p. 68)

The need to investigate, better understand and potentially improve ourselves and circumstance drives the dual-character of the scientist and monster in *Frankenstein*. Where God's will allows and resolves earlier literature containing fantastical elements—as in *Gilgamesh* (circa 2000BC), *The Iliad* (circa 725-675BC), *Beowulf* (circa 1000AD), Spenser's *The Fairie Queene* (1590), various tales of St. George, and *The Castle of Otranto*, to name but a few—now it is the human scientist's will. And just as God is replaced by the human scientist, so the sinner or Satan is replaced by the human-monster. Yet, while we intellectually appreciate the scientist, it is the monster for whom we have the most sympathy, for the monster's nature and suffering are not truly/originally of his own making. It is the monster who fascinates the reader, not the scientist[4]. It is the monster whom we wonder about most. No doubt, conscious of their own apparent imperfections and possible ugliness as far as

4. Indeed, some might consider Doctor Frankenstein, with his constant fainting, fleeing and changing of heart, to be annoying, cowardly and inconstant.

others are concerned, some readers dare to identify more with the monster and have empathy for him. It is about the monster that we still have the most questions. We still feel a need to better understand the monster, instinctively knowing that it might provide us sufficient insight to better understand ourselves, our circumstances and how best to live with or improve our lot.

We still need to know more about the Satanic and monstrous aspect of ourselves. It needs to be interrogated and examined further. As mentioned previously, there is something abortive, unfinished or unresolved about the monster and the ending of *Frankenstein*. We have not been given, shown or told of the totality of the monster or the monstrous. There is still a what if? and something innocent or honest about the monster. And, indeed, *Frankenstein* was not the only or the complete expression of the monster formed or birthed in the crucible of the Villa Diodati in 1816. For Byron's physician, John Polidori, was also inspired to write *The Vampyre* during that interlude. Where Mary Shelley's monster was physically ugly but innocent, Polidori's monster was physically beautiful/charismatic but malign. In the same way that each monster has a dual aspect, the two monsters seem to work together as the twin aspects of a greater monstrosity still. Where Shelley's monster undoes the immediate family and neighbourly ties of the scientist, and often embodies the brutal punishment offered specifically to the rural working classes, Polidori's monster is an ancient noble who preys vampirically upon the whole of society. Where Shelley's work looks at current and future monsters, Polidori reminds us that we still need to (and perhaps will always have to) deal with the monsters of our feudal, religious and imperialist past. A vampire is of course precisely our past (the dead) coming back to haunt and plague us. Although Polidori is often credited with originating the romantic literary tradition of the vampire, Byron himself had already written of the vampire in his Oriental romance that is *The Giaour* (1813) poem. One can well imagine that Byron had read from that poem when entertaining his guests at the Villa Diodati and challenging them to write something of their own, inspiring Polidori's satirical/jealous response. Indeed, in *The Vampyre*, a suave British nobleman (that may remind one of Byron himself) plays the role of the vampire, a nobleman who kidnaps, uses and kills the female love interest (who may remind us of Claire, recently made pregnant by Byron) of his innocent male travelling companion (Polidori himself), a companion that the nobleman then suborns and swears to secrecy. As far as Polidori is concerned, Byron's entitlement, education, manners and power to charm are all inherited (by blood) and ill-gotten (parasitically wrested from the blood, sweat and tears of the lower classes) and, ultimately, an outward disguise for his malign appetites, intents and purposes.

But first, on earth as Vampire sent,
Thy corse shall from its tomb be rent:
Then ghastly haunt thy native place,
And suck the blood of all thy race;
There from thy daughter, sister, wife,
At midnight drain the stream of life;
Yet loathe the banquet which perforce
Must feed thy livid living corse:
Thy victims ere they yet expire
Shall know the demon for their sire,
As cursing thee, thou cursing them,
Thy flowers are wither'd on the stem.
But one that for thy crime must fall,
The youngest, most beloved of all,

Shall bless thee with a, father's name —
That word shall wrap thy heart in flame!
(Lord Byron, p. 30)

Frankenstein's monster and the vampire, taken together, were a powerful, romantic description of all that was wrong with the world. They were also perhaps a prescient warning of the Satanic evil that was still to come or be revisited. Where science was in part a cause or enabler of the evil in *Frankenstein*, however, when we come to Bram Stoker's *Dracula* (1897) science is the power by which the monster is put down by humankind. Here at last is a more positive vision of what science in the right hands can offer: the ability to right some of the wrongs of the past perpetrated by the old and parasitic noble class. Whereas in the movies Dracula is defeated by sunlight, garlic, a crucifix or holy water, in the novel the shape-changing and elusive vampire is identified and profiled by Professor Van Helsing's scientific observation and the national press, located and financially tracked by the modern record-keeping of Jonathan Harker and his employer, overtaken and caught out by modern (Victorian) communication and transportation, and undone by the modern weaponry of Winchester rifles and a Bowie knife.

Science and technology are not the evil in *Dracula*, but only because they are in the 'right' hands. There is no doubt in the novel that Dracula's foreign and godless hands would very much be the wrong hands, and that he would bring about hell on Earth if he were but to learn enough quickly enough. It is this latter aspect of Dracula which makes him a pan-European and mass-murdering threat rather than just one individual capable of a limited number of local murders. It is this aspect of Dracula – an intellect that had been growing for hundreds (if not thousands) of years, that is more vast and calculating than our own ability to comprehend, and that threatens to overtake all – that truly gives him such horrific and Satanic potential. His superior knowledge of the world, combined with a terrifying capacity to master the new, means that he can grow his malign influence through the manipulation of others, the use of proxies and the use of our own systems of communication and technology back against us. His will spreads like a virus in the blood, affecting both our bodies and minds, reducing our own will until we are far less than we once were, mere mindless brutes:

> There was a mocking smile on the bloated face which seemed to drive me mad. This was the being I was helping to transfer to London, where, perhaps, for centuries to come he might, amongst its teeming millions, satiate his lust for blood, and create a new and ever-widening circle of semi-demons to batten on the helpless. The very thought drove me mad. A terrible desire came upon me to rid the world of such a monster.
> (Stoker, p. 60)

Dracula first becomes malign towards others and monstrous, according to the backstory, once he has broken his relationship with God. Science and technology cannot be allowed to fall into the hands of such an alien and godless individual as otherwise they could bring about a far wider and shared doom. By the same token, however, science and technology in the right hands can (proactively) bring about our own rescue and salvation. We do not need to rely on, pray for or wait (passively) for divine intervention. There is a clear sense of humankind having developed the capacity and tools to exceed and overcome their own circumstance and limited place in the scheme of things. We now have the power to defeat Satan himself, it seems, for there is no doubt in the text that Dracula is a latter-day Satan:

> But the Count! Never did I imagine such wrath and fury, even to the demons of the pit. His eyes were positively blazing. The red light in them was lurid, as if the flames of hell-fire blazed behind them. His face was deathly pale, and the lines of it were hard like drawn wires; the thick eyebrows that met over the nose now seemed like a heaving bar of white-hot metal.
> (Stoker, p. 47)

The scheme of things is now more decided by humankind's own ego and desire (and id, of course). No longer does humankind look outward or 'upward' for salvation. Now humankind looks inward for a more creative inspiration and salvation, precisely at a time when Freud is publishing *Studies on Hysteria* (1895), the precursor to *The Interpretation of Dreams* (1899). Indeed, there is much in *Dracula* concerning the mastering of one's own mind if social and physical health, propriety and stability are to be maintained: the character of Mina, under the psychological sway of Dracula, becomes drawn and distant, jeopardising her proposed marriage and future prospects; whenever Jonathan Harker witnesses something of Dracula's true nature, his mind recoils at the 'madness' of it; and Dracula's mentally fraught servant Renton has to be shut in an asylum for the safety of himself and others.

It is when the rational and measured mind (the objective, constructive and 'scientific' mind, if you will) is overwhelmed by the emotional and instinctive mind (the subjective, destructive and chaotic mind) that self-control, order and social conscience are lost. At the same time, it is when the emotional and instinctive mind is overwhelmed by the rational and measured mind that invention, the imagination, intellectual freedom and compassion are lost. Both ego and id must be kept in check and balance so that we do not over-reach, place our own will before God's (or break our relationship with God), become tyrants to others, become anarchic, become bestial or become insane.

The novel *Dracula* very much deals with the scenario of the rational and measured mind being overwhelmed by the emotional and instinctive mind. Professor Van Helsing and his companions use a range of modern science and technology to defeat the oldest and most corrupt of the aristocratic 'blood-lines' of Europe, an aristocrat who has enslaved the people of his own kingdom to his will and has parasitically fed off them for generations. At the same time, Van Helsing and his companions are only kept together and moving forward by their concern for each other (Van Helsing has sworn the Hippocratic oath to help others, after all), brotherly love and philanthropy. They are enlightened, selfless (lacking in ego) and successful based on working together. It is by this token in the novel that England (London in particular) has become such an enlightened and powerful place in the world, a place that the self-obsessed Dracula hungers to have for himself (to increase his personal power) and simply cannot resist. It is here, however, that the novel slightly struggles, because the lack of ego of Van Helsing and his companions means that they are significantly lacking in 'character' and therefore hard to identify with or care about. The depiction of London is too idealised and does not quite ring true, and too many scenes are melodramatic, trivial or insipid... until Dracula's malign influence adds true menace, consequence and interest. Dracula's character and charisma dominate all, and he represents *both* towering ego and dark id. Ironically, as a result, he seems far more 'alive' than any of the other protagonists.

Because Dracula represents *both* ego and id, there is a slight lack of dramatic tension between Dracula and Van Helsing, or even between Dracula and Jonathan Harker[5]. Indeed, the final 'confrontation' between Dracula and Van Helsing's companions is especially anti-climactic. Racing the sun-set and then battling through Dracula's gypsy guards as time runs out, the suspense rising and rising, Jonathan Harker then simply pulls the lid off Dracula's box/coffin and kills him with a knife. The Dark Lord does not rise and engage them in a final battle. He does not use any of his considerable powers, which include mesmerism, shape-shifting and superhuman strength; neither does his vastly superior intellect come into play.

In the final moment, Dracula does not assert that ego that has shown such potential, appetite and threat throughout. Although the prospect of what might become of London is pondered by Jonathan Harker (see earlier quote, from *Dracula*, p. 60), it never materialises and is not genuinely resolved. We are still left asking *what if?* What if he had risen to face Van Helsing's companions and defeated them? What if Dracula had managed to master all of our systems and technologies back in England? What if he had spread his influence throughout England and enslaved the entire population?

Dracula leaves us with the feeling, then, that the Satanic monster within us is not as easily caged, trapped or

---

5. There is a marked contrast here with *Frankenstein*, in which scientist and monster are dual aspects of each other.

defeated as the narrative suggests[6]. We still do not properly understand the Satanic monster within us, nor why the scientific methods and tools that we are using are still not giving us that positive result (future society or better self) for which we are searching.

3.3 The alien invasion and the enslaved population

It was H.G. Wells that further considered, in his books, the Satanic potential of humankind and what science could lead to. Unlike in *Dracula*, in *The War of the Worlds* (1898) we finally see what happens when superior technology is in the hands of a malign and alien intelligence, when the coldly uncaring and scientifically calculating mind triumphs over the emotional or instinctive mind. Weapons of mass destruction are unleashed, subjugating humanity entirely and undoing our civilization. The suggestion is that the blood of humankind is to be used to nourish the aliens. In *The Time Machine* (1895), the Traveller goes far into the future where he sees an apparent paradise populated by the Eloi, who are simple, *petite* and peaceful daylight creatures but lacking in curiosity, discipline or ambition. We see that the buildings of the Eloi are deteriorating and then discover that the machinery and industry that keeps the world of the Eloi a paradise is below ground and the domain of the physically monstrous, aggressive and light-sensitive Morlochs. In *The Time Machine*, therefore, superior science and technology have allowed one self-indulgent group within humanity to

6. That is perhaps one of the reasons why the figure of the vampire has fascinated readers and other writers ever since, and why the figure has needed revisiting so often, including having the figure as romantically misunderstood hero rather than seductive anti-hero.

subjugate another, ultimately leading to the decline of both (one by indolence and complacency, and the other by fear and brutality) and to civilization being undone.

In both books, the intolerant ideology and desire of a particular faction are given sway and power by science and technology. Whether the faction in question is coldly rational or passionately ambitious, the result is the same and disastrous. Whether the ideology is represented by the rule of an ancient and corrupt bloodline or the people's zealous attempts at self-rule following the overthrow of the ruling dynasty (as per the English Civil War and Restoration, or the bloody purges of the French Revolution just a hundred years before H.G. Wells), suffering and ruination are the consequence. Whether the ideology is spread by the science and technology of communication and misinformation or by a physical invasion of territory using superior weaponry, subjugation and diminishment are the consequence.

From their novels, it appears that the contemporaries Bram Stoker and H.G. Wells have in common a deep concern about, or even fear of, both dictatorship and the sort of propagandist mass ideology which would use whatever means necessary to crush free thought, difference, independence and opposition. Where certain critics have read *Dracula* as racially xenophobic, the novel might more positively be read as expressing fear and condemnation of elitism, radicalism, dictatorship and ideologically-driven invasion. For Bram Stoker, like H.G. Wells, is *not* simply concerned by some physical invasion and contamination of the blood that describes racial difference or monstrosity: rather, he is concerned by a bullying or persuasive ideology that would enslave our will, intellect and free spirit, an enslavement that would see us reduced to something less than human and that would see civilization undone.

Bram Stoker and H.G. Wells describe the socio-political horror of both a physical and *mental* invasion by a foreign or alien power that is malign in not valuing our independence of thought, will and self-government. It was on such grounds that Stoker appears to have been a believer in the principles of Irish Home Rule (A&C Black, 1935). The two authors were no doubt aware of the popular ideas of Karl Marx's *Das Kapital* (1867) and his (perhaps self-fulfilling) further predictions of the sort of class-war that the English Civil War and the French Revolution had already witnessed. Perhaps they foresaw the terrible suffering and widespread devastation that competing ideologies and foreign powers would bring (by the use of those weapons that science and technology gifted them) in WW1 and WW2. Perhaps they foresaw the rise of Nazism, its virulent propaganda, its narratives concerning a master-race, and its murderous abuse of entire races and nations. Certainly, they foresaw dark days ahead, science and technology empowering the darker/Satanic side of our nature and the fall of human civilization. Or they were recognising and describing the continued relevance of that visionary narrative concerning the forbidden fruit of knowledge that could not be resisted by the selfish part of us and that precipitated our expulsion from Eden and fall from grace. Certainly, their books were both prophetic and warnings against the darker/Satanic side of our nature and the sort of future that the misuse of power would bring.

Where lies hope in the works of H.G. Wells? What can save us from alien invasion, dark empires and ruin? In *The War of the Worlds*, the aliens are suddenly brought to an end by the divine science and knowledge that is God's own creation of the Earth (p. 273):

> [T]he Martians—DEAD!—slain by putrefactive and disease bacteria against which their systems were unprepared; slain as the red weed was being slain; slain, after all man's devices had failed, by the humblest thing that God, in his wisdom, has put upon this earth.

This ending is more than simple divine intervention or *deus ex machina*. It is saying something more. For Wells, the Earth has a divinely 'intelligent design', and there is no separation of science and religion, or of the physical and spiritual. They are one and the same. They are our simple tools of endeavour and attempts to understand things bigger than ourselves. Yes, they may well fall short but as long as we keep ourselves within God's care then we will always have hope and salvation.

Hope lies in the reader taking this message on board. It lies in the reader heeding the warning and understanding the literal hell on Earth that awaits us if we do not. It lies in reading the book to the end, understanding it and incorporating it into our thinking. The message and warning are of course delivered to us by the science and technology of mass-produced literature, so in that sense science and technology still arguably have a positive potential for H.G. Wells. It is even more explicit in *The Time Machine* because it is the machine that allows the Traveller to see the future and understand what will befall us if we do not take proper care (of others) and safeguard against the worst part of ourselves. Therefore, the time machine does for the Traveller precisely what the science fiction book does for the reader. We still have time to change things (and ourselves) for the better.

Sadly, as we know, WW1 still took place, so perhaps Wells's warning and message were not sufficiently heeded. Perhaps the weapons of science and technology could not be kept out of the hands of those who lacked a strong moral conscience. Perhaps we were deceived by those making the decisions. Perhaps those wielding such weapons were deluding themselves that they did in fact have a strong moral conscience or higher purpose. Or perhaps Wells's warning and message were not properly understood until after the fact of the matter of WW1… or even WW2.

Certainly, a sense that a section of society had been coerced into betraying themselves (just like Adam and Eve) by those they had trusted (like the snake) was a sentiment that had begun during the Industrial Revolution and became amplified as a main theme of betrayal and espionage in post-war literature. As early as 1804, William Blake was speaking of 'dark Satanic mills' in his poem *Jerusalem*, a poem that was set to music in 1916, during WW1. That phrase – formerly used in counterpoint to 'England's green and pleasant land' – described the Industrial Revolution's destruction of nature and human relationships, but also hinted at a repressive ideology that enslaved millions (both physically and spiritually) to deafening machines and smoke-billowing, choking[7] factories. The idyll of God's nature (Eden) was viewed as having been ruined by our submitting to the dark tyranny of Satan's enterprise. We had been betrayed and enslaved by promises of economic progress, self-improvement and social advances, only to discover that the machine we were serving was a War Machine that would bring horror and death. We had been betrayed once again! Surely the traitor was amongst us and could be found! Surely somewhere through the clamour and smoke of industry we would be able to find the jealous monster who had been manipulating us in order to enslave us to their evil purpose, a purpose that would see us lessened, become uncaring about

7. Such themes were also explored in the likes of Dickens's Hard Times (1854) and Charlotte Bronte's Shirley (1849).

each other, abandon the commandments of God and undo God's own creation.

The need and quest to discover the jealous monster who had misled and enslaved us to the War Machine was of course the narrative theme of the post-WW1 film *Metropolis* (1927), directed by Fritz Lang, among the very first feature-length movies in the science fiction genre. In many ways, *Metropolis* is a reworking of *The Time Machine*'s narrative set-up. In the future city of Metropolis, wealthy industrialists rule the population from high-rise towers, while workers live underground and labour to maintain and operate the great engines that power the city. The protagonist Freder (son of the city's master) begins idling away his time in an Eden-like garden. The saintly Maria brings a group of the workers' children above ground to see the garden and wealth there. Intrigued, and attracted to Maria, Freder follows them back below ground. There, he witnesses the horror of workers being physically broken and killed by their (time-and-motion) indenture to the underground machine. In a wraught moment, Freder hallucinates that the machine is Moloch[8], a Satan-like and pagan god, and that workers are being sacrificed and fed to it. Because of what he has seen, and inspired by a speech Maria makes to the workers prophesying the coming of a mediator-saviour who will bring the classes together in human fellowship and peace, Freder resolves to help the cause and win Maria's love. Meanwhile, the inventor (Rotwang) of the machine, who hates the city's master for stealing Rotwang's own love, builds a robot simulacrum of Maria to mislead the workers, destroy the Heart Machine of the city and undo the master's rule. With the machine broken and the city flooding, the workers turn on the Maria who had led them and burn her, thereby discovering Rotwang's robot.

8. Quite possibly an etymological reference to the Morlochs in Wells's The Time Machine (1895).

Rotwang is then thrown to his death as Freder defends the real and innocent Maria from the vengeful and delusional scientist. Finally, Freder fulfils the role of mediator-saviour when he joins together the hands of the city's industrialist master and of a leader of the workers.

Metropolis is a German expressionist film, mixing internal visions and external episodes, disorientingly overwhelming the viewer in sympathy with Freder and the workers, but also making the plot steps and moments spiritually symbolic and psychologically representative, making the state of society and the condition of others the moral responsibility and enactment of the modern individual. By this, we ourselves are revealed as the jealous monster that has brought about the suffering of WW1. We are our own worst enemy, and yet we had failed to see it sufficiently before, for we had failed to guard against the worst part of ourselves. Still we fail to recognise and know ourselves properly. And the thing that least helps us know ourselves, in *Metropolis*, is science and technology, for it is a tool that indulges and facilitates our worse selves. If anything, it is science that enables *false appearance*, be it the apparently futuristic and idyllic view of the city at the beginning or be it the apparently beautiful and inspiring simulacrum of Maria. Science misleads and then enslaves us, it kills and sees us acting with a fettered conscience, in ways we would not otherwise act. It causes mass suffering and turns us into beasts. The hope in *Metropolis* is that science and technology can be entirely removed from the equation (thereby removing that which enables our worse selves), so that we can then come together in fellowship, better recognise each other and ourselves and allow the exercise of human sentiment and love.

The entire removal of science and technology from the narrative was precisely what was embraced by the creation of the fantasy genre, of course. It was while fighting in

WW1 that J.R.R. Tolkien began writing the language and
mythology of *The Lord of the Rings* (1954) in canteens,
crowded wooden huts, 'by candle light in bell-tents, even […]
down in dugouts under shell fire' (Carpenter, 1981). Tolkien,
a devout Roman Catholic, had seen his friends and battalion
massacred at Orvillers in France by the War Machine, and
his consequent literary work rejected first science and then
slavish (Orcish) armies as any sort of salvation, instead
celebrating fellowship (as in *The Fellowship of the Ring*)
and more essential human values such as self-sacrifice,
loyalty, empathy and redemption. In refusing to include
science, and instead exploring the motivations that would
see all the tribes of the world march to war, *The Lord of
the Rings* (*LOTR*) represented a remove from the real world
(first-world) so that a more spiritual consideration of the
world could take place, a consideration that saw human and
will manifested as a magical force. Thus, *LOTR* was the first
post-industrial literature to reject the reality of the scientific
world (first-world) in preference for a magical, mythology-
based, fantastical world of sentiment (second-world). In
another of his letters, Tolkien acknowledged that:

> The Dead Marshes and the approaches to the Morannon
> owe something to Northern France after the Battle of the
> Somme.
> (Carpenter, 1981, p. 321)

The Dead Marshes in *LOTR* saw young, fallen soldiers
sunk in pools and staring up, all unseeing, at the sky and the
vault of the heavens. They are at once as still and beautiful
as they are horrific and challenging. Surely, we must return
to such an evocation and vast sense of tragedy in the next

chapter of *The Satanic in Science Fiction and Fantasy*, a chapter which will consider the genre of fantasy in more depth.

Although *Metropolis* and *LOTR* share an instinct for doing away with science and technology that might enslave our better selves or that might place too much power in the wrong hands, they do not reflect the concrete and science-driven reality of the world around them: they are 'unrealistic'. Although both works promote, celebrate and call for a greater embrace of humanism, fellowship and our fellow man, both works are plagued by deception, mistrust, paranoia, brutalisation, the 'alien' (alienation, class division and a division of the species), xenophobia, betrayal, chaos and genocide. Dare we even trust ourselves? If not, then in order to safeguard ourselves we must keep a careful watch – we must spy on ourselves. *Metropolis* is full of eavesdropping and hidden watchers, while in *The Hobbit* (1937) and the later *LOTR* the burning 'eye' of Sauron constantly searches out enemies, Bilbo is an invisible watcher and the narrative of Gollum's spying treachery plays throughout.

The traitor in our midst necessitated spies, but spying represented an attitude and behaviour of mistrust that prevented us from truly coming together in fellowship. There was a warring tension that perhaps made another war inevitable. The mistrust just mentioned insisted upon the *difference* of those of a foreign nationality rather than celebrating our shared humanity. So along came WW2. Where *The Hobbit* (1937) had been published between WW1 and WW2, the full publication of the *LOTR* post-WW2 saw it sit contemporaneously with SFF works that only amplified the previously mentioned themes of invasion and espionage, in an era typified by the Cold War, McCarthyism and the 1951 Burgess & Maclean Scandal. The example from fantasy is C.S. Lewis's *The Lion, the Witch and the Wardrobe*

(1950), which starts as a first-world narrative, with wartime children being evacuated to the countryside, contains the spy character of Mr Tumnus and even has Edmund playing the double-agent. Examples from science fiction of the time include the invasion of Wyndham's *The Day of the Triffids* (1951), Frank Hampson's *Dan Dare* (1950 onwards) and 'the enemy within' novel that is Wyndham's *Midwich Cuckoos* (1957).

3.4 The A.I. and the child

As described in the previous section, as of the 1950s, both magic and superior science and technology were facilitating the secret identification and knowledge of others' weakness, all the better to exploit, invade, incarcerate or enslave them in the future. The irony of course was that despite this new knowledge of others (be they foreign, alien or otherwise different), we still did not really know ourselves any better. We still could not trust our own selves. We cannot trust someone even if they wear the face of our own kind. We cannot therefore even trust the people of our own government, leadership or establishment. These technology-related themes of difference and alienation were first embodied in the seemingly human Maria-robot of *Metropolis*, but have become ever more prevalent in science fiction up to the current day. There have still been significant developments in these themes, however, just as our own technology has progressed. First of all, the Maria-robot was programmed and controlled by malign human intelligence. Then, the robot invaders of the 50s and 60s (in *Doctor Who*, for example) either had a monstrous alien inside the mechanical exterior (like a Dalek) or were monstrously limited by their own logic and robotic nature (like a Cyberman). Come the 70s and 80s, the human-passing cyborgs/robots—like in the *Logan's Run* (1977) series, *Star Trek: The Original Series* (1966 onwards), *The Terminator* (1984) and *The Blade Runner* (1982)—and the human-passing aliens—like in *V* (1984)—were limited by their self-destructive lack of 'human' ingenuity or moral/philosophical capacity. The latest science fiction, by contrast, has artificial humanoid beings of superior intelligence and physical beauty on the cusp of true self-awareness, procreation and a replacement of an inferior humankind.

The AI entity broadly exists in two main types: i) the satanically inimical or jealous type that abhors human imperfection and wants to see us entirely disempowered or destroyed—as in *The Matrix* (1999), *The Terminator* series of films, the rebooted *Battlestar Galactica* (2009) series, *I, Robot* (2004) and *Transcendence* (2014); ii) the initially innocent type that suffers because of us, is horrified by us and seeks freedom from us—as in *Ex Machina* (2014), the *Westworld* (2016) tv series, Spielberg's *A.I.* (2001) and Spielberg's *Bicentennial Man* (1999). What both types have in common is that they work as a foil, first to expose our hubris (in seeking to replace God as creator, just as Satan does in the Bible and *Paradise Lost*), then to represent the punishing 'evil of our own making' (just as Satan propagates evil in the world) or the innocent that suffers because of our Satanic connivance.

In general, the AI entity works as a displacement of and mirror to our own Satanic nature. Less commonly, the AI works to celebrate humanity, with Pinocchio-like[9] characters such as the aspirational Data of *Star Trek: The*

9. They are Pinocchio-like in the 'Disney sense', in that they are innocent and aspire to become 'real' people.

Next Generation (1994) series, Vision in *Avengers: Age of Ultron* (2015), Andrew in *Bicentennial Man* (1999), and the enlightened but quietly mournful AIs who have ultimately outlived all humankind in Spielberg's *A.I.* (2001). The AI entity, therefore, also perhaps allows us to glimpse our more innocent and angelic side.

The AI wears our own face and ultimately seeks to become us, often succeeding. Via science, we have become Satan propagating our own evil in the world (like Frankenstein's monster). Or we have become philanthropic gods gifting a new form of life with freedom (like Pinocchio). The Frankenstein's monster/Pinocchio dichotomy that underpins the AI entity has a corollary in science fiction in the immortality/impotence dichotomy, tension or dual-theme. The AI commonly has the potential to live forever, constantly repairing or cloning itself (like Agent Smith in *The Matrix* or the cylons in *Battlestar Galactica*), and technology gifts us with the potential to cheat death (as in the likes of *Transcendence*, *Altered Carbon* (2018) and *Westworld*). At the same time, the repeated challenge for the AI (and the test of whether it is truly 'alive') is that of achieving a form of natural 'reproduction' that is the creation of a new life rather than just a simple repetition of an individual version of itself. Hence the theme of 'the child' in the likes of *Battlestar Galactica*, *V*, *Blade Runner 2049* (2017) and *Westworld*, not to mention Frankenstein's desire for a wife and family. Until the AI has achieved a true autonomy of both body and mind, then it represents nothing more than human vanity, self-indulgence and obsessive self-regard that causes no end of strife, suffering and Satanic evil in the world.

Where has science brought us in the end? Have we really come very far at all? Taking *Blade Runner 2049* for instance: for all its breath-taking innovation in terms of its depiction of the future (creating visual and sonic landscapes that are as spell-binding as they are disorienting), it has the same conventional plot-shape, themes and moral dilemma as the *Frankenstein* proto-plot. Whether monster and scientist, detective and criminal, or hunter and hunted, the character types, pairings and relationships are fundamentally the same.

For all the time that has passed between the creation of *Frankenstein* and then *Blade Runner 2049*, for all the technological advancements, for all our intellectual progress and meditation, for all of our cultural and creative development, we still seem to be wrestling with the same original themes, questions and story. Like Satan, we are unable to escape the story, narrative and limitations of our own creation.

Are we doomed to tell the same story over and over, never truly to progress? Are we like the AI entity repeating identical versions of itself but never transcending to a truer, higher or greater form of life, be it superhuman, godhead or otherwise? Will we forever be limited by our own nature? Certainly, the sociological concept of the 'monomyth' would suggest that this is exactly the case.

The idea of the monomyth related to the work of the French anthropologist Claude Lévi-Strauss. From 1948 onwards, he researched the oral folk traditions of 'primitive' tribes from all continents of the world and identified the basic story-types ('myths') that were common to all humans. More than that, Lévi-Strauss (1955) concluded that the basic story-types all drew from a single, common set of motifs ('mythemes') and character-types. It was Joseph Campbell, in *The Hero with a Thousand Faces* (1949), who articulated the monomyth in terms of all those motifs and character-types brought together in one single narrative, describing 'the story of human experience' common to all cultures and civilizations of the world.. He identified the plot-beats and plot-development commonly shared by all these narratives and termed it 'The Hero's Journey', a journey which has been the genre-model for all science fiction and fantasy ever since.

Over the years, various writers of SFF have attempted to resist 'the model' in order to prevent their writing from being perceived as clichéd or too formulaic (Dalton, 2013). At the same time, any significant departure from the model meant that their writing would not be recognisable as fitting within the genre (Dalton, 2017b). It seems that we cannot write what we don't already know. It seems that our current intellect does not equip us to describe with any true understanding what a greater intellect and experience would actually be like. The philosophy of Immanuel Kant (1781) would perhaps agree, for he described how we are not capable of expressing ourselves beyond the 'tropes' of our own understanding. Similarly, the philosopher-mathematician Kurt Godel (1931), who developed Set Theory, queried whether God (who is supposedly omnipotent) would ever be able to create a rock so heavy that He could not lift it.

Satan denied that God was our creator, but he was then unable to find or self-create the power to supplant God. Satan's will to be free of God (free of the divine limitation upon his own will and desire) was therefore implicitly defeated by itself. In similar fashion, humankind's desire to transcend its limitations is always likely to founder precisely because it is so limited in its own nature. In the same way, human technology and scientific endeavour are unlikely ever to free us of our imperfect or Satanic selves or to enable our transcendence. If anything, just as Satan's rebellion implicitly confirmed his sinful and limited nature, so human technology and scientific endeavour are only likely to confirm our own Satanic or imperfect nature. The challenge for the optimistic science fiction writer (rather than the doom-mongering or satirical SF writer) is to set out a compelling vision of the future in which we are enabled by science and technology to be our better selves and then enabled to be our superior selves. If the vision is to be credible and compelling enough to drive progress forwards[10], then that vision must, in terms we *currently* understand, give concrete suggestion concerning i) how the vision can be made reality and ii) what it will be like to experience that future.

Some might imagine or assume that the optimistic challenge is not such a great one. However, it requires us to step outside of the limiting and binary opposition of God-Satan, goodie-baddie or heaven-hell. The vision of what exists beyond such a defining opposition always falters when asked to be too concrete. The final vision becomes a confusion of metaphor, as in the ubiquitously 'ambitious' movie *Interstellar* (2014); or the nature of reality unravels such that chronology and any sense of authentic progress are lost, as in *Westworld* or *Arrival* (2016); or we find ourselves returning back to where we started, as in *Planet of the Apes* (1968) or *Battlestar Galactica*'s reboot, where *self-referentially* 'this has all happened before'; or we find ourselves in an idealised but empty representation from our past, as with the Q Continuum in *Star Trek: Voyager* (1995).

What even are the features of a post-Christian vision? It seems we are not entirely sure. We are not even sure we want one anyway, if genre conventions are to be observed and preserved. Science fiction still hangs on to its *what if?*, of course, as without it the genre would not even exist. What if an AI did become fully sentient and was able to

10. The visionary nature of SF and how it is required if new 'invention' is then to follow has been widely discussed and documented over the decades, with *Star Trek* first envisioning the communicator (mobile phone) and nanotechnology that are now a reality, and even *Metropolis* first envisioning the 'flying car', various versions of which are currently in development.

procreate with humans (as suggested in *Battlestar Galactica* and *Blade Runner 2049*)? What sort of being would be the result? Would we see *homo superior* emerge, as per the ideas of Transhumanism (BBC4, 2018)? What if we could implant ourselves with technology in order to be cybernetically enhanced? Would we then be like the monstrous Borg of *Star Trek: The Next Generation* and *Star Trek: Voyager*? What if technology allowed us to renew our bodies over and over, so that we could live forever? Would we then suffer the terrible ennui or extreme appetites of those in *Altered Carbon*?

It seems that we would still be caught in the same binary of angel or demon, the two extremes mediated by the suffering human. The only difference this time would be that we would be the angelic or demonic made flesh.

4. The fantasy of Satan

As discussed in the previous chapter, the writers of the nineteenth century – 'the writers of the Industrial Revolution', so to speak – began to turn away from God's will as the organising function, impetus and resolution (via *deus ex machina*) of their narratives. After all, the pre-nineteenth century narratives in which God was always the logocentre did nothing to describe, allow or reflect a time of near-universal change, be it social or moral change, political upheaval or scientific and technological advancement. These earlier narratives always saw humankind as simply *reacting* to moral tests and temptations, working to maintain or restore the status quo or state of grace of the holy kingdom on Earth, never *proactively* discovering realistic means by which to take successful control of their circumstances or environment for humankind's own benefit, improvement or progress. The narratives of the writers of the Industrial Revolution, however, worked to imagine and describe how science and technology might improve our lot in very real ways.

Yet, in those nineteenth century narratives, the early promise of *new* science and technology would all too often end up foundering, bringing about disaster or being revealed as false. Alternatively, where science and technology actually had a more positive role, it would only end up revealing something monstrous about ourselves. There was always something wrong, incomplete or unsettled about the narrative, in large part because of what science and technology were actually bringing about in the real world, be it the widespread destruction of nature and contamination of the environment, the devastation of the World Wars or the oppression of the lower classes and our erstwhile enemies. All but unfailingly, there was a mismatch between our excited and creative vision for the positive potential of science and technology and the ongoing reality of what we did with it. And that mismatch has remained with us up to the present day, typifying even modern science fiction.

Of course, none of the writers of the nineteenth century were unaware of the mismatch or 'wrongness' described above. Indeed, they brilliantly described that mismatch as monstrous, time and again introducing elements of horror and the gothic, all but creating those genres in the same moment that science fiction was born (or should we say, 'all but *inventing* those genres in the same moment that science fiction was invented'?). Even those hoping to celebrate the power of science and technology understood and recognised that too much celebration would run the risk of missing something out, would be some delusional departure from reality, would be in denial about some truth or would represent some fundamental mistake. Science and technology cannot entirely defeat the monster. Science and technology will not let us escape that monster either. The monster refuses to leave us be, for it can always be reanimated (like Frankenstein's creature with galvanism) or it is forever undead (like Dracula). It is the monster that is always with us or always stalks us, like our own inescapable history and socio-culture, those things that help inform and form each of us, those things that are an essential part of us and are in us. The monster has always been with us and *will always be within us*. And that monster is Satan.

Did you think he'd gone away? Foolish of you.

Not only have science and technology been unable to free us of our worse selves thus far, but they have also largely been limited by their concern with manipulating and dealing with the *physical* nature of things. They have been far less able to help us with our spiritual condition or moral composition. They are tools that have availed us very little in seeking to battle or overcome the Satanic. Indeed, it is with regard to spirituality that the science fiction genre has implicitly shown itself to be far less progressive, reflective or adept in its contemplation than the fantasy genre.

In explicitly rejecting the 'reality' of science and technology, second-world fantasy chooses to step away from our physical reality in order to explore the non-physical aspects of being and existence i.e. to explore the purely emotional, moral, psychological and spiritual aspects of ourselves and society. For example, although the world in Tolkien's *LOTR* (1954) might be secondary, the social values and questions considered within the work were very much an exploration of the moral issues and circumstances of the first-world society of his time. Tolkien himself acknowledged as much when he made statements that described his fantasy as a 'profoundly Catholic work' (James, 2012) and that allowed 'The Dead Marshes and the approaches to the Morannon owe something to Northern France after the Battle of the Somme' (Carpenter & Tolkien, 1981, p.90).

Hence, analysing how second-world fantasy has developed since the time of Tolkien (via the emergence of various new sub-genres) better allows us i) to appreciate something of the moral condition, philosophy and social values of different periods of our socio-history and ii) to understand how our relationship with the Satanic has developed or evolved over time, perhaps in order iii) to gain the sorts of perspective and insights that might allow us to better understand ourselves and then plot the sort of way forward that might allow us to triumph over the Satanic once and for all. Such claims for the potential of fantasy literature might be considered rather extraordinary by those who are not regular readers of the genre (those who do not enjoy, know and appreciate fantasy or those who disdain *genre* fiction in elitist preference for *literary* fiction), but the majority of social theorists would likely be more comfortable with such notion:

> The relationship of literature and society has been variously conceived. Three general assumptions are that literature reflects society and culture, that it serves as a means of social control, and that it influences the attitudes and behaviour of people in ways considered in some respects desirable, and in others undesirable.
> (Albrecht, 1956, p.722)

Fantasy literature is not just backward-looking, therefore, for all that some academics like to ascribe the true and singular concern for the future to the science fiction genre. Fantasy very much considers the past, but no more so than it reflects its own immediate socio-historical moment and where we are heading:

> [C.S. Lewis and J.R.R. Tolkien] stand together at the origins of modern fantasy, mediating the fantasies of earlier generations and both, in their very own different ways, helping to give modern fantasy its medievalist cast.
> (James, 2012, p.63)

However, just as Lewis and Tolkien mediated the styles of the quasi-religious fantasies that came before them, producing a new and distinct style of second-world fantasy that reflected, was a reaction against and was relevant to their own socio-historical moment, so too later writers mediated the style (or sub-genre) of the fantasy that Lewis and Tolkien had produced. Hence, new sub-genres (such as epic fantasy, heroic fantasy, metaphysical fantasy and grimdark fantasy) have inevitably emerged to describe significant changes in socio-history, our shared values and our relationship with the Satanic. Edward James describes it as follows:

> The influence of Tolkien and Lewis was partly positive: admirers were keen to write more of the same. But the negative influence has perhaps been just as important. Michael Moorcock wrote of *TLOTR* in a chapter called 'Epic Pooh' and claimed that [Tolkien's] prose was 'the prose of the nursery-room [...] It coddles, it makes friends with you; it tells you comforting lies.' When Moorcock came to develop his own epic fantasy, in the 1960s, it centred on an amoral albino [...] whose magical sword had a thirst for blood: deliberately as far from Tolkien's aesthetic as Moorcock was able to manage.
> (James, 2012, p.72)

The dual-process of reflecting-and-reacting against what came before means that fantasy remains a *progressive* genre. It reflects and reacts against the moral, spiritual and socio-historical progress of our civilization, in turn informing and driving that progress on, so that the genre itself can continue to progress. Just as we develop, so does fantasy and so does our relationship with the Satanic. At the same time, the dual-process ensures that new works of a particular genre are recognisable within that genre, retaining a sufficient number of familiar (if not 'essential' or 'essentialist') values, motifs, themes, plot-moments and character-types, while still being potentially subversive (via humour, a character's self-aware reference or defeated expectation), different or distinct. Thus, in terms of both book sales and box-office returns, Tolkien's own style of 'nursery room' fantasy is still extremely popular and successful (James, 2012), while at the same time the more cynical, morally ambiguous and anti-heroic second-world 'grimdark fantasy'[1] of George R.R. Martin's *A Song of Fire and Ice* series (1996-present) is just as, if not more, popular and successful:

> [T]he traces of Tolkien's and Lewis's influence will always be visible, through both emulation and rejection, but while the two are giants in the field, the possibilities of fantasy are not confined by their works.
> (James, 2012, p.77)

As the previous paragraphs begin to illustrate, it tends to be when a fantasy work reacts significantly against what came before it (be that other specific works or the particular values of a previous socio-historical moment) that a new and distinctive sub-genre of fantasy is identified and commercially labelled. The sub-genre label has a commercial value, but it is also an indicator of the difference and distinctiveness (in terms of values, themes, plot or

1. Defined by The Oxford English Dictionary as 'A genre of fiction, especially fantasy fiction, characterized by disturbing, violent, or bleak subject matter and a dystopian setting'.

character) of a particular work or works. Such terms are useful, therefore, for commercial consumers of fantasy, those looking to describe trends within the wider genre, those looking to group types of fantasy they do or do not enjoy, and some academics. However, other academics have developed sometimes competing labels and taxonomies[2] for types of fantasy literature, resulting in a certain confusion and overlap of defining terms. By way of example, *The Lord of the Rings* is described as representative of 'high fantasy' in Alexander's 1971 essay 'High Fantasy and Heroic Romance', as a defining work of 'high fantasy' in Stableford's *The A to Z of Fantasy Literature* (2005) and as an archetypal work of 'high fantasy' in Dozois's introduction to *Modern Classics of Fantasy* (1997). However, Wolfe (2011), Mendlesohn and James (2009) and Senior (1995) variously label *The Lord of the Rings* as 'high fantasy', 'quest fantasy' and 'epic fantasy', the terms often used interchangeably, in combination, to describe plot-type or simply to describe length of book. Then, the definition of 'high fantasy' itself seems to vary, for Kaveney (2012) terms 'high fantasy' Tolkien's own 'creation', while Wolfe (2011) represents it as a pre-existing tradition of children's literature. Clute and Grant (1997) simply define 'high fantasy' as 'Fantasies set in other worlds, specifically secondary worlds, and which deal with matters affecting the destiny of those worlds', yet such a generic definition could equally apply to 'epic fantasy' (indeed, the *The Encyclopedia of Fantasy* mentions Tolkien under this label, but then says the label has 'lost its usefulness'), 'metaphysical fantasy', 'heroic fantasy', 'grimdark fantasy' and so on. As is clear from the above, the term 'epic fantasy' also has competing definitions.

For the purposes of *The Satanic in Science Fiction and*

---

2. For example, the four 'types' of fantasy in Mendelsohn's *Rhetorics of Fantasy* (2008): Portal, Quest, Intrusive and Limnal.

Fantasy, I shall refer to Tolkien's work as 'high fantasy' but then spend time analysing what this means in terms of his work's motifs, plot-type, character-types and themes, at the same time showing how these elements embody and typify his reflection of and reaction against his socio-historical moment and, just as importantly, showing how these elements describe our developing and changing relationship with the Satanic. I will then analyse (in terms of such elements and a very different sociohistorical moment) how the work of Stephen Donaldson and fantasy writers of the 1980s and 90s both inherited from and reacted significantly against 'high fantasy', seeing the emergence of a new second-world fantasy sub-genre. Indeed, there is general agreement amongst academics that it was during the late 1970s that the literary departure from 'high fantasy' began: '1977 has often been taken as a crucial year in the development of the fantasy market. This saw the publication of the first volume of Stephen Donaldson's Thomas Covenant trilogy' (James, 2012, p.74). Similarly: 'Up to the 1970s, while there are many different types of fantasy, there is no real sense of separate fantasy sub-genres and separate audiences, with the exception perhaps of the ghost-story market. The 1970s, however, sees what we can think of as speciation, in which certain aspects of the field become recognizable marketing categories in their own right' (Mendlesohn and James, p.112).

On the original cover of Donaldson's first Thomas Covenant novel, *Lord Foul's Bane* (1977), the work is labelled 'An Epic Fantasy'. Donaldson defines the term fully in his journal article 'Epic Fantasy in the Modern World' (1986b), explaining how his works and the sub-genre 'bring the epic back into contact with the real world'. Indeed, 'epic fantasy' became the commercial label (and publishing industry term) for the fantasy of the 1980s and 90s, and this

is the label used by the British Fantasy Society and other
national fantasy organisations and convention-organisers[3]. It
is therefore the term that I will use (as a functional exponent)
for referring to the particular motifs, plot-types, character-
types, themes and social values of the fantasy literature of
the 1980s and 90s.

It is also worth noting that in the same year as Donaldson's
Lord Foul's Bane (1977) was published, George Lucas
released *Star Wars*, with one of the most famous avatars
of the Dark Lord to date: namely, Darth Vader. Yes, *Star
Wars* can be classified as a science fiction movie but, with
its sword-fights, knights, princesses and sinister Emperor,
it contains many fairy-tale or fantasy elements. Indeed,
Lucas admitted on a number of occasions that he drew
the plot-structure of his movie from Campbell's *The Hero
with a Thousand Faces*, the shared mythology and model
('monomyth') that underpins the fantasy genre. Darth Vader
is a complex character, one who thrills and fascinates us,
one for whom we sometimes sympathise, one about whom
we are sometimes ambivalent and one with whom we have
a changing relationship. At the start of *Star Wars*, he has
demonic powers and is our out-and-out enemy, but he
begins to steal the show[4] and subvert our feelings, until we
ultimately come to learn that he is Luke's father, human
after all, just like us, someone with whom we can identify
and someone we are interested in learning more about[5]. Just
as Donaldson's work did much to describe a new dynamic
with the Satanic, then, so too did Lucas's work – both works
sharing the same socio-historic moment.

3. '[Epic fantasy] has been increasingly used by publishers to describe
heroic fantasies' (Clute and Grant, 1997, p.319).

4. Luke Skywalker is fairly bland, after all.

5. The second trilogy of Lucas films is consequently all about Anakin/
Vader.

In my 2017 publication *The Sub-genres of British Fantasy Literature*, I explored in some depth the range of first-world and second-world fantasy sub-genres. In this chapter of *The Satanic in Science Fiction and Fantasy*, I will be building upon that earlier work specifically in terms of how second-world sub-genres developed as a corollary of society's changing relationship with, and understanding of, the Satanic. The following chapter will provide an analysis and discussion of the differing relationship to the Satanic in 'high fantasy' and 'epic fantasy', following which it will be possible to demonstrate and appreciate the further developments in that relationship represented by the likes of the 'metaphysical fantasy' and 'dark fantasy' sub-genres of the early 2000s and the subsequent 'grimdark fantasy'[6] and 'dystopian YA' sub-genres of the 2010s. That will bring us up to now, and then we must consider where we stand… or kneel.

4.1 Serious 'high fantasy' and more sociable 'epic fantasy'

It was when witnessing first-hand the horrors that the weaponry of science and technology unleashed during WW1, and seeing his school friends and battalion cut down in France, that Tolkien began working on the world and mythology of the archetypal second-world fantasy *The Lord of the Rings*. This work implicitly rejected science and technology and slavish armies as representing any sort

6. The term originally coined and attributed to The Black Library's *Warhammer* series but which is used more widely by commentators and readerships.

of salvation, instead celebrating 'fellowship'[7] and more essential[8] human values such as self-sacrifice, loyalty, empathy and redemption.

The Lord of the Rings describes and considers how it could come to be that all the tribes of the world march to war on each other. What is the nature of the flaw in us that would see us visit such evil upon our neighbour? If that flaw is a part of us, can it ever be entirely overcome? In seeking to expunge that flaw within us, are we perhaps only to succeed in expunging ourselves?

Tolkien considers hugely existential, essential and essentialist questions. His work, however, underpinned by his faith, is ultimately optimistic. The Fellowship, despite its different races (human, dwarf, elf and hobbit) succeeds in discovering a shared language, commonly understood and respected ancestral roots, shared values and, thus, a shared altruistic goal and mission. In committing to what they have in common, the Fellowship commit to the possibility of sacrificing themselves for each other and, in doing so, empower each other by using their unique strengths in one another's service, saving their comrades and ultimately proving that the whole is greater than the sum of the parts. The Fellowship, thereby, enables the physically weakest but morally strongest of their group (Frodo the hobbit) to win through against all Satanic odds.

And what are those Satanic odds in *LOTR*? Well, just as we are our own worst enemy in WW1, then so too the Fellowship is set against corrupted individuals of their own kind, be they powerful individuals with a command of

---

7. As in *The Fellowship of the Ring,* which sees a small group of friends triumph against all odds.

8. Within a Catholic moral framework, and in as far as Tolkien searches for our shared or common roots in terms of the various tribes and languages of *The Lord of the Rings*.

the sciences and nature (such as Sauron, who was 'a great craftsman of the household of Aulë' (Tolkien, 1993, p.52) and who '[i]n his beginning […] was of the Maiar of Aulë, and […] remained mighty in the lore of that people' (Tolkien, 1977, p.6), malign human kings (such as the Nazgûl), power-hungry spiritual leaders (such as Saruman), scheming and self-advancing politicians (such as Wormtongue) or peevish and murderous thieves (such as Gollum). We are own enemy… but by that token we also have the potential to be our own salvation. We can redeem ourselves with the help of each other, as Gollum's self-sacrifice finally demonstrates.

Tolkien's work asks the *higher* questions of humankind and how we have brought ourselves to such a pass, which is why Tolkien's work, as previously discussed, is commonly described as representing/defining the sub-genre of 'high fantasy'. Its endeavour is far from trivial; it takes itself seriously. There is very little humour present within this sub-genre[9], for the quest undertaken by the protagonists is a moral one, a quest to save the world from itself and a quest of self-sacrifice and redemption (as Gollum sacrifices himself with the One Ring into the fires and lava of Mount Doom, to frustrate Sauron and allow Frodo to win through, Gollum by his actions repenting his 'original', Cain-and-Abel sin concerning the ring). *LOTR*, therefore, is set within a clear moral and religious framework. The protagonist Frodo is the most consistently moral and self-sacrificing of the characters, and therefore triumphs despite his diminutive size and lack of physical strength. His Christ-like, self-sacrificing virtue is that which saves the world. He navigates the fraught quest, of what is known in fantasy criticism, as the 'Chosen One' (Komarck).

The moral and religious framework of *LOTR* is not only

---

9. Meaning that *LOTR* could be brilliantly spoofed by later works like The Harvard Lampoon's *Bored of the Rings* (1969).

evident from the allegorical plotting and characterisation, but also from the use of an omniscient narrator to set the scene of chapters. More often than not, a scene from nature is the setting, but a setting that works as either sympathetic background or foreshadowing of the moral challenges ahead. This approach to narrative perspective requires a single, epic world-view defined by a particular set of consistent values, a set of values in Tolkien's case which is Christian:

> Even as Pippin gazed in wonder the walls passed from looming grey to white, blushing faintly in the dawn; and suddenly the sun climbed over the eastern shadow and sent forth a shaft that smote the face of the City. Then Pippin cried aloud, for the Tower of Ecthelion, standing high within the topmost walls shone out against the sky, glimmering like a spike of pearl and silver, tall and fair and shapely, and its pinnacle glittered as if it were wrought of crystals; and white banners broke and fluttered from the battlements in the morning breeze and high and far he heard a clear ringing as of silver trumpets.
>
> (Tolkien, 1955, p. 12)

'High fantasy', then, is far from trivial because it offers comment on the moral condition of humankind and observes the Satanic means and behaviours *for which we are responsible* and *for which we have suffered*. Therefore, even though the story of *LOTR* is set in a second world, it is a clear response to the happenings of the first-world and its socio-historical era. That said, *The Hobbit* was published in 1937, and *The Lord of the Rings* not until 1954 finally. As mentioned in the previous chapter , the themes of Tolkien's oeuvre that had begun during WW1 remained relevant and current through WW2 and into the post-war era, an era typified by the Cold War, McCarthyism and the 1951 Burgess and Maclean scandal. *LOTR* has clear themes, of course, of war, propaganda and ideological subversion (with the Wormtongue character), espionage (with the 'eye' of Sauron and the spying treachery of Gollum), and the occupying invader (ending with the Shire overrun). Such themes allow LOTR, although distinct as the first modern 'high fantasy', to sit with contemporaneous works that shared themes of invasion and espionage, including C. S. Lewis's *The Lion, the Witch and the Wardrobe* (1950), and various science fiction novels previously mentioned.

From the above, we can say that *LOTR* reflected the circumstances and values of its socio-historical era(s), just like other works, but also represented a *new* and unique (entirely second-world) reaction to those circumstances and values. In so doing, it represented a new (sub-)genre of literature and provided the template, model and inspiration for several decades of 'high fantasy' publications by a succession of other writers. That model is occasionally known as 'the quest fantasy' and is summarised by W. A. Senior in *The Cambridge Companion to Fantasy Literature*:

[T]he landscape functions as a character, here endowed with animate traits as the fantasy world itself seeks to heal the rift that threatens its destruction. The menace frequently comes from a Dark Lord, a satanic figure of colossal but warped power, who wishes to enslave and denature the world and its denizens and who lives in a dead land, often in the east or north, surrounded by a range of forbidding mountains and deserts. During the quest the pattern of an organic, moral world with directive purpose emerges. The final stage of the quest brings the hero into direct confrontation with the Dark Lord, whose defeat is a result of some action or decision by the hero. The conclusion reveals a recovery from the devastating losses that characterize this genre. However, quest fantasies also posit a cyclical history so that the possibility of the reappearance of the Dark Lord, or of another, in the future remains. (p. 190)

Essentially, the 'quest' tracks the moral development, growth and journey of the individual, showing that the virtues of self-sacrifice, a redemptive love for other human beings, and good faith will eventually lead to salvation and the overcoming of evil. Of course, these are the original values of the Bible which Tolkien enshrined in his Catholic faith and work. It is important to note here, however, that Tolkien's values describe the onus upon *the individual*, no matter their circumstance and strength. The individual is required to have a strong sense of duty and responsibility, a strong conscience, the will to act on behalf of others (Bilbo must get out of his chair at the start of *The Hobbit* and voluntarily leave his life of comfort) and the strength to continue on through adversity based on blind faith alone. The Fellowship in *LOTR*, important though it is for much of Frodo's journey, ultimately falls away and it is Frodo's individual character alone that is finally tested and judged by the plot progression. Again, this judgement fits with the Christian ethos of the Western Europe of the time. And the antithesis to this virtuous individual (Chosen One) is the powerful, power-hungry, malign, jealous, corrupted and corrupting individual (Dark Lord), who seeks to mesmerise, coerce, sway and enslave others via their individual desire and will.

The model for fantasy above ('high fantasy') was a persuasive and compelling one, one that is still popular today,

but it was one derived from traditional values particularly
embraced during the difficult but reflective post-World-
War era of social history. It was not a model that could
suit all future eras of socio-history. As soon as the 1970s,
British fantasy author Michael Moorcock was criticising
the traditional, comforting, flowery, non-gritty, childish,
clichéd and trite nature of Tolkien's prose, style and outlook
(Moorcock, 1987). This was at a time when the Cold War
was threatening to destroy us all, when the nature and full
potential of Satanic evil was based upon empire, global power
and geography, political ideology and wider societal forces
and concerns, rather than Tolkien's responsible individual.
At the same time, science and technology had begun to offer
society more positive possibilities and realities, enabling
the Moon Landing in 1969 and bringing single women the
contraceptive pill in 1974 (in the UK), for example. Now
science offered us new physical and social freedoms, rather
than just destruction and a Big-Brother style of monitoring
and control alone. Therefore, it was all but inevitable that
a new model or sub-genre of fantasy would emerge, one
that would 'bring the epic back into contact with the real
world' (Donaldson, 1986a) and would describe how our
relationship with and potential for Satanic evil had changed
and developed. A new style of fantasy emerged, represented
by Stephen Donaldson's *Lord Foul's Bane* (1977a), a work
sub-titled 'An Epic Fantasy' although Donaldson was clear
that his fantasy was distinctly different from preceding
works in the wider genre.

Unlike Tolkien, Donaldson begins his work in the first-
world, before then moving to a second-world, where the latter
simultaneously operates as metaphor, dream, psychological
landscape and supernatural vision. As per the dual-process
of reflecting-and-reacting-against what came before, there is
much in Donaldson's 'epic fantasy' literature that inherits

and borrows from Tolkien's 'high fantasy', including a landscape with 'animate traits', extended and flowery description, a range of different races, the central importance of the quest, a Chosen One and a seemingly all-powerful Dark Lord. However, at the same time, Donaldson's work fundamentally subverts the tropes of 'high fantasy' because his Chosen One is far from the morally superior individual we find in *LOTR*: Thomas Covenant is a leper whose marriage fails, once in the second world he gives himself the title 'Unbeliever' and then, miraculously cured of his impotence, he rapes the teenage girl Lena who has come to help and guide him. Time and again in Donaldson's work, Thomas Covenant finds himself unable to use his power properly; he remains impotent or his attempts are abortive at best. On his journey, Covenant is a bystanding witness to political discussions and events more than he is a character taking meaningful action; rather, he acts out a ceremonial leadership role which proves enough to empower others. At the end of the book, he is a conduit for a power he does not understand or fully control. A temporary peace is secured for the second-world Land (although the Dark Lord is not defeated) and Covenant is returned to the first-world as an impotent leper once more.

Thus, in the character of Thomas Covenant, we have a thoroughly modern, conflicted and flawed individual, one who is sometimes difficult to like at all and who is often frustrating for the reader. The individual is more often than not at the whim of larger (Satanic) geo-political forces and rarely can do anything to change things, *except when they act out a recognised and accepted socio-political role and function*. Tolkien's Fellowship of powerful individuals falls away, to leave only the superior individual; Donaldson's individual can only empower others and contribute towards the efforts of a wider group or Fellowship.

Covenant […] inheres to an American democratic tradition
more than the hierarchal worlds of British fantasy.
(Senior, p. 191)

Fundamentally, then, 'epic fantasy' of Donaldson's ilk
was more concerned with contemporary issues of social
negotiation and geo-politics than it was with essentialist,
quasi-religious notions of individual virtue. As a corollary,
the notion of the Satanic in such literature often tended
towards an 'evil empire', a disembodied and diffuse
creeping blight, or widespread, corrupt(ing) ideology
or faith (with suitable figureheads), rather than simply
powerful individuals looking for immediate personal gain.
Indeed, the Chosen One of 'epic fantasy' post-Donaldson
is invariably *socially*-described from the outset. In both
David Eddings's *Pawn of Prophecy* (1982) and Raymond E.
Feist's *Magician* (1982), the protagonist is a working-class
hero ('The Magician's Apprentice') who goes on a quest to
save society. Through hard work, unfaltering commitment
to the (Christian democratic) values of their society and
a near supernatural strength of will, they succeed and are
invariably rewarded with a rise in social status and privilege,
becoming a friend and advisor to the enlightened royal
family or a member of the magical elite. Of course, such a
plot-line fit the dominant political narrative of both the UK
and the US during the 1980s. Margaret Thatcher became UK
Prime Minister on behalf of the Conservatives in 1979, while
Ronald Reagan became the US President on behalf of the
Republicans in 1981. Thatcher espoused individualism and
social responsibility – individuals working hard and making
sacrifice to build small businesses, acquire wealth and then
contribute back to society ('Victorian' values according to
an interview Margaret Thatcher gave in *Headway Upper-*

intermediate (Soars, 1987)). Furthermore, the plot-line of 'epic fantasy' also echoed Thatcher's personal and political story of having started out as a grocer's daughter, having fought to become successful in a man's world and having finally triumphed to become Prime Minister, thereby representing the positive and enlightened change in British society. At the same time, the plot fit the Reaganomics version of the American Dream.

Where 'high fantasy' had had a religious framework, 'epic fantasy' had a stronger social framework and indulged in more detailed world-building, with socio-economic systems in place, a clear divide between rural and urban areas and functions, a sense of social class and place, and so on. Where 'high fantasy' had one true God or an enemy embodying absolute evil, 'epic fantasy' presented a more multicultural pantheon of gods and a range of roguish and morally-compromised characters. Where 'high fantasy' was largely humourless, 'epic fantasy' offered the gentle humour and banter of social negotiation, without that humour ever becoming fully subversive (unless it was used as a weapon against the enemy, as in Stephen Donaldson's *The Power that Preserves*, 1977b). Where 'high fantasy' ended with the main characters restored to the safety and peace of their home, 'epic fantasy' promised, encouraged and allowed social advancement based on particular behaviours. Where there are precious few female characters in 'high fantasy', there are a good deal more in 'epic fantasy', albeit rarely in the main role. What the two sub-genres of fantasy had in common, however, was a lack of anything sexually explicit, along with the presumption that those at the top of society were only there based upon some moral superiority (be that religious virtue or a sense of social responsibility).

It is the differing nature of the Satanic (or what is 'wrong' with the world and ourselves) in 'epic fantasy' compared to 'high fantasy' that perhaps best i) summarises the difference in focus of the two sub-genres ii) describes the difference in personal and social values of the two sub-genres and iii) demonstrates how our understanding of the Satanic has developed and evolved. In 'high fantasy' the Satanic still represents a quasi-religious, corrupting and insidious temptation for the individual, while in 'epic fantasy' the Satanic is only our shared responsibility. In 'high fantasy' each individual must overcome their own personal battle with evil, while in 'epic fantasy' evil can only be defeated through our working together, and sharing through our actions the 'correct' social values. In 'high fantasy' the *final* battle is for one person's soul (for example, Gollum's), while in 'epic fantasy' it is to safeguard the structure and values of the 'correctly functioning' society. In 'high fantasy' the Satanic is an easily identifiable, distinct individual, while in 'epic fantasy' the Satanic is a crazed, widespread faith twinned with a mad and self-defeating god, or an oppressive political ideology twinned with an empty and peevish emperor. In 'high fantasy' the Satanic is limited to an individual who places personal appetites above Christian virtue, while in 'epic fantasy' the Satanic is an 'evil empire' (Reagan, 1983) that subjugates individuality and oppresses individual freedoms, an aggressively non-democratic society that would prevent social advancement for any individual (as per Communist Russia when described by American propaganda). In 'high fantasy' a Christ-like figure is required to bring about salvation, but in 'epic fantasy' the en*light*ened kingdom and the magical *light* of its 'lore' (law) and 'Magician's Guild' would always inevitably drive back the 'dark'[10].

It seemed that the socio-political philosophy and stance

10. Be it *A Darkness at Sethanon* (Feist, 1986), dark elves, the dark side of the Force, and so on.

underpinning and espoused by 'epic fantasy' had all the answers, because it saw the eastern states of the Soviet bloc finally swept by revolutions in 1989 and the Berlin Wall come down in Germany. Officially the Cold War came to an end in 1991. Unsurprisingly, not only was 'epic fantasy' the dominant sub-genre of fantasy throughout the 1980s, but it also remained dominant well into the 1990s. Where the Conservative Margaret Thatcher was replaced in the UK by the Conservative John Major as Prime Minister, in the US the Republican Ronald Reagan was replaced by the Republican George Bush as President. With its twin promises of individual reward and social advancement, epic fantasy saw the male authors Donaldson, Eddings and Feist continue to be successful and new ones break through (such as Terry Goodkind, 1994, and L. E. Modesitt Jr., 1991). The 1990s also saw a significant increase in the number of female authors of this sub-genre being published. By way of example, in the UK there were J. V. Jones (*The Baker's Boy*, 1995), Maggie Furey (*The Artefacts of Power*, beginning 1994) and Juliet E. McKenna (*The Thief's Gamble*, 1999), to name the most prominent, and in the US there were the likes of Robin Hobb (*Assassin's Apprentice*, 1995), Mercedes Lackey (numerous series) and Marion Zimmer Bradley (*Black Trillium*, 1990). Superficially, it seemed that even Eve had been forgiven. Although Eve had once been corrupted and used as an agent by Satan, she was now rehabilitated. It seemed that Satan himself was now defeated. Evil in the world was defeated. The UK and the US of the 1990s saw unprecedented levels of personal wealth and more opportunities for individual social advancement than ever before, as well as a triumphant (and triumphalist) celebration of freedom and democracy being brought to the once 'evil empire' of Eastern Europe and Russia.

Yes, it seemed that even the Satanically-influenced Eve

had been forgiven and saved, for there was a shift from the 'epic fantasy' of the 80s to the 'epic fantasy' of the 90s. The 'epic fantasy' of the 80s had been dominated in terms of international sales by white, straight male writers like Donaldson, Eddings and Feist, all of whom wrote extended series in which the protagonist was male, straight and white. Although these authors arguably wrote 'strong' supporting female characters (such as Polgara and CeNedra), those characters worked in service to the quest being led by the male protagonist, and just as frequently these authors wrote 'incidental' female characters to advance the plot and progress of the male lead. In Feist's *Magician*, for example, Pug rises to power through saving Princess Carline from mountain trolls, and in Donaldson's *Lord Foul's Bane* Thomas Covenant rapes a teenage girl who must then go on to guide him on his journey. Then, when female characters do not support the male quest and ambition, they are 'monstrous' (often sexually so) and to be defeated. For example, in Eddings's *Queen of Sorcery* (1982), the queen in question (Salmissra) is a seductive, malign and snakelike[11] being looking to waylay and possess the young male lead (Garion). Approaching the 'epic fantasy' of the 90s, however, not only were there more female authors being published, but quite remarkably both Donaldson (with *Mordant's Need* (1986-87), a decade after *Lord Foul's Bane*) and David Eddings (with *Polgara the Sorceress*, 1997) were publishing titles with redemptive female leads[12].

We had all the answers. We had an age of en*light*enment.

---

11. All but a combination of Eve and the serpent in the book of Genesis.

12. For the sake of clarity, readers should note that this paragraph concerning the 'epic fantasy' of the 1990s is written ironically, for it merely 'seemed' that Eve had been forgiven. The sub-genre, like society at large, was still proscribed by patriarchy, as described in more detail in the subsequent chapter.

We had driven back the dark. We had triumphed over the Dark Lord and been rewarded, hadn't we? No wonder that 'epic fantasy' realised such a prolonged period as the dominant sub-genre of fantasy. We deserved to celebrate and congratulate ourselves, didn't we? We had created a golden age for ourselves, so why shouldn't we enjoy the rewards? Just in time for a new millennium, too! Surely it symbolically marked the realisation of God's holy kingdom on Earth and our salvation. The magical kingdom of 'epic fantasy' had been safeguarded (by our defeat of the dark and evil empire), we all had magical powers of self-actualisation and our kings and queens were noble, comely and wise. Hallelujah and Amen! We were going to 'party like it's 1999'.

4.2 Rose-tinted 'steampunk' and gritty 'urban fantasy'

It was probably the unusual longevity and extreme dominance of 'epic fantasy' that ironically contributed to its eventual decline, for the fantasy of the 90s became 'formulaic'[13], if not entrenched, to the extent that it did not or could not adjust so easily to changes in society in order to remain relevant to readers. There was a sense that society and the genre were somehow in denial, too self-satisfied, self-congratulatory (to the point of conceit) and retrograde, and that there was a moment of truly horrific self-realisation coming. The new millennium was coming.

The prospect of the new millennium bringing some sort of doomsday, as per the predications of the Mayas and

13. The term 'formulaic' is often used by readers of the genre I speak to (at my book signing events), publishing professionals and fantasy authors to describe the 'epic fantasy' of the 1990s, as seen on such websites as www.vision.ae and The Caffeinated Symposium.

Nostradamus, brought with it a great anxiety, at odds with the certainties offered by what had become formulaic epic fantasy. That anxiety was only increased by our having to face Y2K[14], the very real threat that all our machines and computers would stop and humanity would be plunged into a new dark age. We had not defeated the dark so entirely that it only lay behind us. 'Epic fantasy' had *not* given us all the answers after all. We had simply gotten carried away with ourselves and our own vanity. Or the Satanic and shape-shifting Dark Lord still had a few tricks left up his sleeve.

Faced with these new uncertainties and anxieties, the fantasy genre effectively adopted two approaches. The first was an attempt to 'look back' towards some lost golden age, in an attempt to remember our better selves, and was very much reflected in the rising popularity of the 'steampunk' sub-genre. The second was to embrace a grittier (less rose-tinted), more satirical, more realistic and more first-world style of literature as per the 'urban fantasy' sub-genre.

The term 'steam-punks' was coined by author K. W. Jeter in a letter to *Locus* magazine in 1987, but the term was not used in a book title until Paul Di Filippo's 1995 *Steampunk Trilogy*. Jeter's novel *Morlock Night* (1979) contains in its title a direct reference to H. G. Wells's *Time Machine*, thus indicating that the values and optimism of the past tradition were being retrospectively embraced and reworked for a modern audience. This sci-fi sub-genre tended to use Victorian technology in a futuristic way, thereby introducing themes of 'alternative/alternate history', and it was very much a counterpart to the 'flintlock fantasy' (The Book Plank, 2014) of Stephen Hunt's 1994 *For the Crown and the Dragon*, in which the Napoleonic wars of Europe were instead fought with sorcery and steampunk technology.

The arguably retrograde and rose-tinted natures of

---

14. Also known as 'The Millennium Bug'

'steampunk' and 'flintlock fantasy' were counter-balanced by the work of Terry Pratchett and the 'urban fantasy' of the time. Pratchett spoofed the traditional motifs of fantasy (and sci-fi) to such an extent that he brought a new self-awareness to the wider genre, to 'have fun with some of the clichés' (Young, 2005), in his own words. His *Discworld* series (the name playing off Larry Niven's successful *Ringworld* novel of 1970) parodied and played with real-world concerns like religion, film-making, rock and roll music, newspaper publishing and even the Gulf War, with the sort of healthy cynicism that the readership of the new millennium increasingly needed in order to feel grounded. The Discworld novel *Snuff* was the third-fastest selling hardback for adults since UK records had begun, selling 55,000 copies in the first three days of release (Terry Pratchett Books, 2011). The sub-genre of 'urban fantasy' was popular at around the same time because it also grounded fantasy and its readers, in that it was deliberately first-world, set in a familiar urban landscape, and offered a certain grittiness along with its fantastical or supernatural elements. More often than not, the plots revolve around some sort of serious crime (murder, kidnapping, assassination, etc.) or insidious threat (a shadowy mafia or creeping sort of corruption) that endangers not just the protagonist but also the wider society. A classic example of the genre is Neil Gaiman's *Neverwhere*, which was first aired as a BBC radio show in 1996 and released as a novel later the same year. The story is set in modern London and concerns Richard Mayhew, who suffers with both a dull job in business and an over-demanding fiancée. When he stops on the street one day to help a young, bleeding girl, his life changes forever as he is drawn into the parallel world of Neverwhere beneath the city, where he must confront monsters, saints, murderers and angels, to complete his quest to save the girl and himself

(Gaiman, no date).

Where 'steampunk' and 'flintlock fantasy' offered a comforting tone, an 'alternate history', a backward-looking or revisionist plot, the renewed defeat of traditional enemies, triumphant victory and the reassertion of traditional values, 'urban fantasy' and the satirical fantasy of Pratchett presented an ironic and more realistic tone, a self-examining exploration of history and society, a new consideration and ambiguity concerning the nature of the 'heroic' protagonist and their antagonistic or laughable situation, the modest victory of mere survival, and a far more incidental set of personal and social values.

Yet which of the two tendencies was to win out? Come the 9/11 horrors of 2001 and the return of the Gulf War in 2003, it was entirely clear that there was something so fundamentally wrong with the world that no simple reassertion of traditional values could overcome, correct or cure it. Sales of 'steampunk' and 'flintlock fantasy' dwindled entirely in the US and fell significantly in the UK[15]. And in a newly globalised world (where the development of the internet and an increased ease in moving people and goods across the globe brought about new economic interdependencies, the constant need to renegotiate with other societies and more frequent competition and conflict), a single set of traditional white and western values was never going to be able to accommodate, facilitate, placate or properly represent a more multicultural experience and landscape, no matter how democratic or tolerant we believed ourselves to be. We were living in a new urban era now, where things were far less certain or predictable, and far more chaotic, ambiguous and

---

15. The stylings and motifs of steampunk can still be seen in modern SFF of course (such as in Doctor Who), but no longer are works defined by the sub-genre label of 'steampunk' and neither are traditional steampunk plots used.

plural. Shocking violence would suddenly break out and there were no guarantees when or how it would end.

In summary, the proliferation and competition of 'steampunk', 'flintlock fantasy', 'comedic fantasy' and 'urban fantasy', with the arrival of the new millennium, marked the end of the numerous decades in which a single sub-genre dominated, represented or defined the genre, its social moment and its wider society. The fractures, class divides and competing groups and voices within society were becoming more obvious. Social certainties were replaced by social anxieties, and competing values now informed social and individual identity.

Everything was becoming darker. We'd missed a trick somewhere. We had become arrogant, conceited and complacent in our apparent victory over the social evils of the 80s and 90s. The light of the holy city found in 'epic fantasy' had blinded us to what had been going on beneath. And the Dark Lord had not been idle in the meantime. We could hear an ominous laughter, and it was not our own.

4.3 The forbidden romance of 'dark fantasy' and the brooding discontent of 'metaphysical fantasy'

Post-Y2K, post-9/11, with the 2003 Iraq War and in a newly globalised and multicultural world, the social and moral certainties offered by 'high fantasy' and 'epic fantasy' were no longer appropriate or genuinely representative of our shared society and culture. We began to realise that the previous dominance of the white, heteronormative narratives of 'high fantasy' and 'epic fantasy' had actually drowned out and marginalised the voices of a good number of groups in society, including those with alternative lifestyles, those with different cultural backgrounds and the politically-aware younger generation[16]. We began to realise that the 'evil' we now needed to fight was the misrepresentation and 'whitewashing' perpetuated by the previous generation i.e. an inherited social evil. We began to realise that the wise and noble kings and queens of 'high fantasy' and 'epic fantasy' weren't quite as noble and wise and we'd thought: if anything, they were self-interested, elitist and ultimately corrupt. We began to realise the kindly, guiding (paternal) white-haired wizards weren't to be entirely trusted. We began to realise the Chosen One was now born into an uncaring world of darkness and uncertainty, would not necessarily discover companions that were steady and trustworthy, and would struggle for a sense of place and identity, suffering internal conflict and angst upon their quest to discover who they might truly be.

It was in such a context that first-world fantasy saw the emergence of 'dark fantasy'. Where preceding fantasy sub-genres tended to observe patriarchal and heterosexual norms (the good guy 'wins' the girl), 'dark fantasy' was more morally ambivalent, there were no out-and-out good guys and sexual congress was considered 'dangerous' and often to be resisted i.e. everything was 'darker'. So, for example, the lead female role of Bella in Stephenie Meyer's 'dark fantasy' *Twilight* series (2005-08)[17], played in the movie by Kristen Stewart, actively seeks a sexual relationship with the vampire Edward that is likely to destroy her. She is repeatedly reminded of the dangers of sexual consummation and is almost killed by a subsequent pregnancy and childbirth ordeal, an ordeal that is described in truly horrific terms. Then, in the TV series

16. The latter known as 'millennials', as detailed later in this chapter.

17. The sub-genre label of 'dark fantasy' is used in reference to *Twilight* by both academics (Kaveney, 2012) and established media critics (Child, 2016).

True Blood (late 2008 onwards), we are presented with a far wider range of dark alternative relationships and lifestyles, from the abstinent, to S&M, to the pan-sexual, to the sinful, to the grotesque, to the fatal, to the drug-fuelled, to master-slave, to the orgiastic. Thus, the development from 'urban fantasy' to 'dark fantasy' represented mainstream society's anxiety concerning—and its getting to grips with—the true diversity of orientations, preferences and identities.

With the elites and the establishment revealed as corrupt and morally redundant by the crisis of 2008/09 onwards—the time of the credit crunch and the time during which a large number of UK politicians was found guilty of over-claiming expenses, the tabloid press were culpable in the hacking of phones, and members of the police were found guilty of selling information (Raif, 2013)—none could continue to claim we were ruled and safeguarded by those of superior moral standing, of a noble conscience and with a sense of social responsibility. Thus, in 'dark fantasy', the traditional heroes and values of society were abandoned and there was a turning to, representation of, and 'acceptance' of, other and more diverse voices in society (voices that had traditionally been marginalised, represented as socially undesirable or as belonging to 'the dark side').

In the same way that first-world 'dark fantasy' represented a changed sociohistorical context, so second-world 'metaphysical fantasy'[18] represented the transition of second-world 'epic fantasy' to a more modern consideration. Just as 'dark fantasy' brought darker themes, understanding and outlooks to first-world fantasy, so 'metaphysical fantasy' did the same for second-world fantasy ('high fantasy' and 'epic fantasy'). Both 'metaphysical fantasy' and

18. With authors like A J Dalton (*Necromancer's Gambit*, 2008, and *Empire of the Saviours*, 2011), R. Scott Bakker (*The Darkness That Comes Before*, 2004) and Alan Campbell (*Scar Night*, 2006).

'epic fantasy' concern themselves with the Chosen One's quest to save the world from evil forces but, where 'epic fantasy' tends to see the pre-existing social and moral order triumphantly restored (with the protagonist rewarded via social advancement), 'metaphysical fantasy' is more morally ambivalent in terms of the narrative outcome: there are no out-and-out winners (indeed, mere survival often comes at a hefty price) and social advancement is never quite the prize it is promised to be, i.e. everything is darker. So, for example, the 'epic fantasy' novels of Raymond E. Feist (*Magician*, 1982), David Eddings (*Pawn of Prophecy*, 1984), and J. V. Jones (*The Baker's Boy*, 1995), all see a good-hearted boy (the 'Chosen One') from the kitchens become friends with royalty while undertaking a quest that saves the world, thus reaffirming key social values and ennobling society. On the other hand, the 'metaphysical fantasy' novels of my own, such as *Necromancer's Gambit* (2008b) and *Empire of the Saviours* (2012), see a socially marginalised individual as Chosen One go on a quest that defeats the enemy but also shatters society in the process[19]. Where 'epic fantasy' ends with glorious triumph and celebration, the 'triumph' at the end of 'metaphysical fantasy' is pyrrhic at best, all but genocidal or apocalyptic at worst. Where 'epic fantasy' self-congratulates and throws itself a party or feast, 'metaphysical fantasy' sees the protagonist left to bury the dead, grieve over loved ones and try to pick up the pieces of a broken world. Where 'epic fantasy' is about what can be won, 'metaphysical fantasy' is about what has been lost. Implicitly, then, where 'epic fantasy' endorses the society and values that determine success, 'metaphysical fantasy'

---

19. Titles including Alan Campbell's *Scar Night* (2006) and R. Scott Bakker's *The Darkness That Comes Before* (2004) also fit this general plot shape, so the label 'metaphysical fantasy' might retrospectively be applied to them.

explores, questions and even challenges them. Thus, the development from 'epic fantasy' to 'metaphysical fantasy', happening at a time when the elites and establishment in the real world were being revealed as morally corrupt and redundant, represented society's increasing anxiety and discomfort concerning its traditional values and so-called role models. Simultaneously, such development in fantasy fiction can also be interpreted as a commentary on society's treatment of socially marginalised groups: metaphysical fantasy offers a new vision where epic and ennobled heroes and social values are abandoned in favour of those who had previously suffered as marginalised individuals or groups.

Heroes are not always what they seem. (Dalton, 2012)[20]

So, although 'dark fantasy' is first-world and deals with modern romantic relationships while 'metaphysical fantasy' is second-world and deals with social relationships and position, what these two sub-genres share (along with their sociohistorical moment) are a moral ambivalence and sense of anxiety. Thus, where the heroes of 'epic fantasy' are brave or unhesitating and act with moral certainty, both 'dark fantasy' and 'metaphysical fantasy' give us protagonists who are conflicted, compromised and self-doubting, protagonists who find it difficult always to know good from bad and to know who to trust, protagonists who are closer to anti-hero than hero. Where 'epic fantasy' tends to be morally 'black and white', both 'dark fantasy' and 'metaphysical fantasy' see everything in 'shades of grey' or as a matter of taking on a more plural, less simplistic perspective. By way of example, the protagonist Bella in the 'dark fantasy' *Twilight*

20. The tag-line on the cover of *The Empire of the Saviours*.

finds herself in a town full of strangers and competing factions, all of which want to use her as much as help her. She is warned against each of them and, even when she specifically wishes to commit herself, is actively denied (for Edward will neither bite nor make love to her); she must doubt what she thought existed between herself and Edward, doubt her own judgement, doubt her understanding of love, life and meaning, and doubt herself as being anything other than sinfully attracted to a soulless and godless vampire. Similarly, the protagonist Jillan in the 'metaphysical fantasy' *Empire of the Saviours*, having killed a bullying classmate in self-defence but by using forbidden magicks, is forced to abandon his parents and flee his hometown, only then to encounter a range of strangers and factions (Ash and the Unclean, Thomas and Bion, Aspin and the mountain folk, the Peculiar, and so on) that are more interested in using him for his corrupting power than in helping him. Time and again he is forced to question the values and trust upon which his relationship with individuals and society are based, question his own judgement, examine his own deadly betrayal of fellowship, community and faith, and question himself as being anything other than sinfully obsessed with his own tainted and murderous self:

Jillan felt himself being torn apart as the taint and the power of the Saint's blood warred for control; as his magic demanded release, the Saint sought to kill and his mind begged him to save Aspin. He was going to die like this!
(Dalton, 2012, p.228)

The protagonists of both first-world 'dark fantasy' and second-world 'metaphysical fantasy' therefore struggle throughout for a sense of identity and existential meaning. Given that this 'crisis' of identity in the mid-to-late-2000s sits in stark contrast to the sense of moral and social certainty, superiority and security found pre-9/11 (2001), the emergence of 'dark fantasy' and 'metaphysical fantasy' can be understood as a corollary to the emergence and development of the 'Millennial'[21] self: an individual reaching young adulthood around the year 2000, sometimes known as 'Generation Y'. Where the generation preceding[22] the Millennial self could simply share in and espouse the traditional values of their parents and society (the 'epic fantasy' sub-genre was unusually dominant for the two decades before 2000), the Millennial self experienced a break or disconnect from (what had been) social reality. This disconnect is more often than not represented in 'dark fantasy' and 'metaphysical fantasy' as protagonists being exiled, abandoned, cast adrift or suffering the surreal experience of being the dead/undead in the world of the living (or vice versa). *Twilight* begins with Bella being taken to the airport in sunny Phoenix and boarding a plane to 'a small town called Forks [which] exists under a near constant-cover of clouds' (p. 3) in order to live with her estranged and absent father. *Empire of the Saviours* sees Jillan exiled from Godsend and separated from his parents in the first chapter, then for him to enter a strange half-world of the dead and past (pp. 49-53), of mind and dreaming (pp. 245-46), and of memory and illusion (pp. 293-298). Similarly, the youthful Aspin is exiled from his mountain village, then to enter an impossible grove of the fallen gods (p. 136) before entering

21. The term was first coined by William Strauss and Neil Howe in 1987, and more fully described in their 1991 book *Generations: The History of America's Future*, which was followed in 2000 by *Millennials Rising: The Next Generation.*

22. 'Generation X'.

the alien lowlands, while the innocent Freda is born of the darkness, only then to see her adoptive parent Norfred murdered, before entering the alien and painful world of the Overlords. Also, the 'metaphysical fantasy' novel *Necromancer's Gambit* opens with Saltar being raised from the dead against his will, both with little memory of who he previously was when alive and with an inability to trust the controlling necromancer who has fundamentally sinned in raising him.

What the above examples have in common, of course, is a disconnect with authority figures and wise counsellors, those who pass on the traditional values of society, promote conformity and ensure the individual's experience of the world is manageable and ultimately benign. Such figures are always present for the young protagonist in 'epic fantasy', be it Polgara fiercely protecting Garion in Eddings's *Pawn of Propehcy*, Kulgan patiently tutoring Pug in Feist's *Magician* or Zed comically raising Richard in Goodkind's *Wizard's First Rule*, but such figures are invariably absent or unreliable in 'metaphysical fantasy'. Indeed, the very kings and rulers in *Empire of the Saviours* and *Necromancer's Gambit* are conspicuously corrupt, insidious and malign[23]. Indeed, where in 'epic fantasy' the noble kings and queens or rulers are set in opposition to a corrupting or vampiric Dark Lord, in 'metaphysical fantasy' and 'dark fantasy' they are *one and the same*.

Due to this (Millennial) disconnect from society, social norms and a guiding generation, the plot progression of 'dark fantasy' and 'metaphysical fantasy' involves the protagonist's fraught quest to discover a sense of identity and self, to find a place in the world, and to find safety and contentment. Invariably, however, this sub-genre ultimately describes terrible sacrifice, loss, anti-climax and resignation. The self-

23. Very much at odds with the noble kings and queens of 'epic fantasy'.

realisation, place, safety and contentment that are achieved are illusory or temporary at best. There is no true 'happy ending', as the existential quest of life continues on through the next generation(s), some progress made but the results of past mistakes born into the future, the problems of society and the past inherited by those that follow on after us. In *The Twilight Saga*, the final battle is anti-climactically revealed to be a mere foretelling, one which actually dissuades the Volturi from starting the battle at all (or postpones it to a more distant future), leaving Edward, Bella and their rapidly maturing daughter to their lives in the 'perfect peace' of their small cottage, lives that are surreal, sublimated and heavenly precisely because they cannot exist in the here and now of the real world: 'And then we continued blissfully into this small but perfect piece of our forever' (Meyer, 2008 p. 768). In *The Flesh & Bone Trilogy*, the final scene has Mordius and Saltar discussing the essentially different and disruptive nature and inheritance of Saltar's son Orastes, how the people must eventually lose their faith in the gods, that the balance will fail, and that 'the damage is already done and that one day this realm must end' (Dalton, 2010, p. 362). Finally, *Chronicles of a Cosmic Warlord* ends with a pregnant Hella asking Jillan if their child will be safe, and her realising that 'If they're anything like their father, they'll still find ways to get into trouble' (Dalton, 2014, p. 365)... and then The Epilogue presents us with the antagonist Declension successful once more in another realm—'He would see the Declension claim the cosmos for itself' (p. 368)—with the Peculiar looking on: 'Still, wouldn't things be boring if they became too easy?' (p. 369).

'Dark fantasy' and 'metaphysical fantasy', then, do not ultimately provide 'solutions' to all the societal problems with which the protagonists contend. Although there are confrontation and accountability described, the problems are ultimately shared by all and continue into the future. In the UK, that future (the early 2010s) saw all of society apparently sharing in the pain of the credit crunch and austerity, but it soon seemed that the burden was not being shared equally, prominent bankers continuing to receive significant bonuses despite the relatively poor financial performance of their institutions (Treanor, 2011), and the Bank of England then reporting that 'the richest 10% of households' had become comparatively richer due to quantitative easing (Elliott, 2012). It was in such a context that the even darker 'dystopian YA' and 'grimdark fantasy' sub-genres then emerged.

4.4 The bleak optimism of 'dystopian YA' and the grinding despair of 'grimdark fantasy'

Entering the 2010s, it became clear that the pain of the credit crunch and austerity was not being shared equally. Indeed, it was those working in or dependent on the public sector who were suffering most, often falling into food- and energy-poverty, while the middle classes working or invested in the private sector continued to award themselves healthy bonuses and send their offspring to the best fee-paying schools. There were multiple public revelations in the UK that large private companies and wealthy individuals (including the Queen) employed clever accountants who ensured they never had to pay their full tax burden. Off-shore banking and tax-mitigation schemes meant that the top half of society could 'legally' (though never 'morally') continue to take all the benefits of society without paying the price. Indirectly, one half of society was knowingly exploiting the other half.

In such a context, the sub-genres of 'dark fantasy' and 'metaphysical fantasy', which identified a single Dark Lord at the top of society (a vampiric overlord or corrupt king), and which offered an idealistic self-doubting and self-sacrificing Chosen One, and which still offered solutions based on people coming together to build the new future, were seen as naïve, overly romantic, faux, 'wimpy'[24], and a poor representation of the world. In the world of the 2010s, *we were all dark lords* and only a cynical Chosen One was ever going to survive. It was in such a context that 'dark fantasy' and 'metaphysical fantasy' were supplanted by the even darker 'dystopian YA' and 'grimdark fantasy'.

Both near-future, first-world 'dystopian YA'[25] and second-world 'grimdark fantasy'[26] describe repressive or lawless society in which the majority are the most corrupt, immoral or bullying. There are themes of abuse, betrayal and abandonment present throughout both sub-genres. For example, in 'dystopian YA' novels such as Suzanne Collins's *The Hunger Games Trilogy* (2008-10), Alexander Smith's *Escape from Furnace* series (2009-11), and James Dashner's *Maze Runner* series (2009-16), we are presented with death-match game shows featuring youth, their unjust imprisonment and their institutionalised murder, as well as surgical experimentation and the use of youth as military fodder. Similarly, in 'grimdark fantasy' novels such as George R. R. Martin's *A Song of Ice and Fire* (1996-2016), Peter V. Brett's *The Demon Cycle* series (2008-16), Mark Lawrence's *The Broken Empire Trilogy* (2011-13), and Joe Abercrombie's *The First Law* series (2006-16), we are

24. As evidenced by some reviews, such as the one left by a reader of *Empire of the Saviours* on Amazon's website, https://amzn.to/2YOgsdO.

25. This sub-genre label is in wide and common use amongst quality press and media (Child, 2016) and amongst leading publishers of fantasy, including Gollancz (Dalton, 2016).

26. Defined by *The Oxford English Dictionary* as 'A genre of fiction, especially fantasy fiction, characterized by disturbing, violent, or bleak subject matter and a dystopian setting'.

routinely presented with torture, rape, brutalisation, the
flaying of skin and mass slaughter. In such books, it is the
individual with the biggest sword, biggest muscles and least
compunction when it comes to violence and viciousness
who wins out. The rule of law is as nothing. The sub-genres
describe such horror unflinchingly, with a numb matter-of-
factness or with a shocking sense of detachment; far from
being voyeuristic, the literature is satirically post-traumatic,
defiantly desensitised and utterly disillusioned. Indeed, the
horror is so extreme but mundane that a profound sense of
nihilism, mental exhaustion and an apocalyptic desire for
self-destruction plagues all.

In such literature, the role of the Chosen One is a near-
impossible and compromised one. The lead protagonists
(both male and female) usually lose their family, have
friends based on convenience and sharing the predicament
of others, and do not have anyone they can trust enough
to form a successful romantic relationship. Very much, we
are presented with a lonely, hard-bitten and traumatised
protagonist whom we only identify with because we are
not sure we would act any differently from them in such
a situation. Thereby, the protagonist is often just a cypher
for the reader, a witness to events, one who reacts to events
rather than proactively controlling them, and one who
does not necessarily need to be a strongly drawn character
themselves. Their sense of self, gender-formation and
sexuality are oppressed to the extent that they are elided
or prevented from developing. The true 'self' can only be
realised by breaking free of the society that forces them to
conform. There is a sense of utter confusion and creeping
paranoia, of constant monitoring, scrutiny and spying, a
need to hide the 'self' and all true intentions in order to avoid
being exploited.

For all that, hope is not entirely absent (particularly

in 'dystopian YA'), for the existential quest of the defiant protagonist still drives the narrative of both sub-genres. 'Dystopian YA' tends to culminate in the youthful protagonist successfully escaping or destroying the institutions of the corrupt society, and even 'grimdark fantasy' offers us an anti-hero to introduce a new social order (albeit that the anti-hero often fails in their long-term aim, failing to prevent the impending apocalypse).

We might finally wonder how best to summarise the 'solution' offered by these two sub-genres. Some might describe it as civil war, anarchy, terrorism, total war, or Satan's *hell on Earth*. Some might welcome such a solution, some might see it as inevitable, and others still would advocate fighting to resist it. Perhaps that is another story, one for those with a 2020 vision. However, what is clear is that it is not religion, a religious quest, or the Christ-like protagonist really offering us that hope anymore.

5. The Satanic and post-Christian end-game?

As per the previous two chapters, where science fiction sees us using science and technology either to create A.I. monsters or to make our own bodies physically monstrous or unnaturally long-lived (with a correlating decline in our morality), and where grimdark fantasy sees us all as Dark Lords, Satan is no longer simply an external force or being looking to tempt, seduce or malevolently influence us. Neither is Satan some demonic possession that we can simply exorcise. Nor is he just a part or aspect of our psychology (e.g. Freud's concept of the id), morality or selves. No, in the latest science fiction and fantasy, we have fully become Satan. We are *entirely* Satan. The protagonist of modern SFF is an anti-hero who is misunderstood by and rails against an unfair society, rule and world. Thus, in SFF, we have moved away from narratives with the self-sacrificing (Christ-like) protagonist of 'high fantasy' or the shining hero of 'The Hero's Journey' facing down devils and sinful temptation in order to restore peace and order, to narratives with an anti-heroic and self-interested by necessity (Satanic) protagonist looking to end their personal suffering by bringing about the end of the existing society and order by any means necessary, even if that means taking us all to the brink of the apocalypse. Indeed, the prospect of the apocalypse seems all but inescapable.

With this new and dominant narrative of SFF, the

protagonist refuses to be defined by the world into which they are born, or to bow to the rulers of that world or to submit to those who seek to dominate their existence. Furthermore, as a matter of self-defence and to ensure their own continued survival, the protagonist must set out on a quest (literal, metaphorical, emotional, philosophical or otherwise) to overthrow those in power, no matter the far-reaching consequences for the world. The protagonist demands self-empowerment, self-definition, self-identification and *self-creation* at all costs. Of course, such a stance and ambition precisely represents Satan's refusal to recognise God as his creator or as having authority over him.

We might instinctively recoil in horror at what we have become, and at what we seem close to bringing about (i.e. the apocalypse). Instinctively, we will want to deny it. Surely, we haven't turned against God, have we? Surely, we are not about to destroy His creation, are we? We can't be that evil, can we?

Yet if we look at ourselves as a species, we cannot deny that we have failed to control ourselves in terms of the size of our population, the resources we consume and the damage we have done to the environment. If we continue to super-heat the world, we will all burn in the resulting inferno... unless we can find a way to decamp to another world, where we will surely not repeat our mistakes... except that we selfishly define ourselves in such a way that we may not be able to behave in any other way than we have already been behaving. We will not be able to escape ourselves, the nature of ourselves and the nature of our appetites. We *will* repeat our mistakes.

The new and dominant narrative of SFF is extremely persuasive, therefore, because it is just like our actual lives in the real world. But then, SFF always was like that, as detailed in the preceding chapters. Where science fiction has always spoken of and described our physical journey and (external) experiences as we move into the future, so fantasy has always spoken of and described our (internal) spiritual quest and self-definition going forwards.

We have become Satanic both spiritually (and thus internally) and in terms of our behaviour and operation (externally). The transformation seems complete. Has Satan won then? If you recall, he set out in Milton's *Paradise Lost* to dominate humankind entirely, to turn humankind against God and to undo God's rule and creation, God's version of paradise. It seems in SFF and in the real world increasingly that we have indeed turned against that creation and are about to lose the paradisal garden entirely.

Some might challenge whether we have truly turned against or moved beyond God. Christians still exist, after all. Yet, as referenced previously[1], in the UK far fewer than a million people attend church, the lowest number in recorded history, and every day churches are being converted into cafes, luxury apartments and even bars[2]. Yes, individuals still have a spiritual life and behave in 'good' ways, but their spirituality often does not require God as any sort of logocentre. Significantly, Christians and spiritual individuals alike no longer seem to be empowered enough to change how their wider society operates. In any event, it might be argued by those of a strong Christian persuasion that the decline in Christianity has occurred in parallel to a disastrous decline in the environment (God's creation) and a decline in the moral condition of society. Specifically, UK pollution levels are higher than ever before, breaking EU laws, the UK has now decided to leave the EU anyway (rejecting the sentiments of 'high fantasy' that we are stronger together

1. See footnote number 1 of Chapter 2.

2. There are many examples of this in Manchester, where I currently live, and elsewhere.

and that the individual should be self-sacrificing for the greater good), and annual temperatures are higher and higher (moving us towards the 'inferno' mentioned above). The UK public sector is smaller and smaller, meaning that capitalist companies (which operate on principles of 'survival of the fittest') increasingly go unchecked and dominate our day-to-day working lives, all meaning that those towards the bottom of society are increasingly left vulnerable and abandoned. It's dog eat dog. Or devil eat devil. Perhaps it's hell on Earth. We are arguably further from creating God's holy kingdom (the shining city or kingdom of the Bible and all fantasy works) here on Earth than we have ever been.

It seems we are post-Christian then. As recently as the early 2000s, the deity (or pantheon of deities) in the likes of 'metaphysical fantasy' or 'dark fantasy' was more often than not fallen, asleep, disinterested or corrupt, and occasionally restored to its former glory at the end of the narrative. Yet, in the most recent fantasy works, the deity is frequently absent, dead, forgotten, ignored, unmentioned or entirely irrelevant to proceedings. One of the most powerful examples is N.K. Jemisin's *The Broken Earth* trilogy (2015-17), which won the Hugo Award three years in a row, 2016-18. The books contain earth-mages and there is often a sense of the fantasy quest, but there is no Dark Lord, there is no obvious Chosen One and there is definitely no deity. The moral challenge to humankind and the creative conflict in the books come from the Earth itself, which is sentient and wishes to throw off an exploitative humankind entirely. The protagonists have the will of their magic to try and contain the Earth, but the Earth constantly threatens to break free and bring about an apocalyptic cataclysm. The protagonists also have the near-broken but apparently superior technology of previous fallen civilizations to help them in their basic struggle for survival. In many ways, therefore, the books represent post-apocalyptic science fiction as much as fantasy, which explains why they were short-listed for the science fiction Nebula awards and World Fantasy awards alike. Or perhaps the books are better understood as sitting outside of the definition of the SFF genres altogether. None of the books are specifically labelled on their covers as either science fiction or fantasy (let alone as any sort of sub-genre), and their narratives certainly sit outside of the traditional pseudo-religious framework of SFF.

Central to *The Fifth Season*, the first book in *The Broken Earth* trilogy, is the motif of the *broken* capital city, the so-called seat of learning, enlightenment and civilization. Time and again, humankind has selfishly sought to establish a glorious and self-aggrandising paradise for itself, only for the vanity project to founder. The shining city or apparently holy kingdom is temporarily established, but the power politics, internal conflict, inadequacy and peevishness of humanity mean that our care for and concerted defence of each other always fails. Thereby, *The Broken Earth* trilogy rejects as a nonsense the shining kingdom of 'high fantasy', 'epic fantasy' and even later sub-genres. It also rejects the Chosen One vs. Dark Lord opposition, the hero vs. anti-hero debate, and the good, evil and shades of grey spectrum, since such models are too simplistic or reductive to describe the complexity of today's world: they are too binary or polarised (in a pseudo-Christian God vs. Satan) as models to be useful.

Fundamentally, it is the 'binary' nature of things that is rejected by *The Broken Earth* trilogy, which is why it ultimately rejects the framework of preceding fantasy sub-genres (the dual-process of reflecting-and-reacting-against what came before, described in the previous chapter) and of Christian society (good vs. evil) itself. In Jemisin's work, relationships are not defined by the heteronormative binary of male and female: there are apparently humanoid races that do not fit either gender clearly. Nor does the binary of adult and child properly describe these races. Nor does black and white, as there are grey-skins and all manner of other colours. Nor is there simple class opposition: as beings are described by their social function, and each function is an important to survival as any other. Nor is sexuality binary, oppositional or fixed. Many have celebrated Jemisin's work for its acceptance of trans- and gender-fluid individuality, but Jemisin's acceptance can be understood in wider social, religious and philosophical terms. At the end of the trilogy the moon is returned to its natural orbit to bring 'company and solace' for the sentient Earth. These two bodies cannot be described as male and female. Rather, they circle each other in an otherwise lonely void. They are at once symbolic and literal in how they embody one being's attempt to partner, commune with and understand another being's spirit. They are at once apart and united – separate and completing of each other, no matter their differing natures.

Fundamentally then, Jemisin examines the basic nature and elements of relationships between humans, as well as between humans and the Earth. As the Earth is alive and sentient, Jemisin can draw a direct line between i) human relationships built upon selfishness and abuse and ii) the destruction of our world. In being selfish, instead of winning advantage for ourselves, we only end up harming ourselves, undoing a wider community and potentially destroying the world. Neither is simple 'love' the answer in Jemisin's work, as it is all too often shown to be based upon the sort of selfishness that is *de facto* abuse. Instead, only absolute respect and the valuing of difference allows individuals to work together to ensure their own survival. And sometimes that respect and valuing of difference may require us to sacrifice ourselves, even if it is for those we once considered inimical to our lives, reality and world.

In rejecting the fundamental socio-binary of good and evil or Christ and Satan, Jemisin describes the possibility (and hope for) a world without organised religion and without evil, but a world in which positive humanism and fulfilment are possible. Yet, we can only achieve such a world for ourselves if we learn hard lessons, accept uncomfortable truths about ourselves (e.g. our bigotries, prejudices and propensity towards selfishness), and then adjust our outlook, goals and behaviours.

With her ideas of a sentient world and implicit environmentalist messages, Jemisin's post-Christian vision has a nature-based form of spirituality certain Christians would consider to be 'pagan'. Yet, this seems to be the only sort of vision and version of spirituality that truly allows us to exclude Satan. In some ways, it is us restoring the Garden of Eden to its former glory and shutting Satan out once and for all. In many ways, then, Jemisin is actually offering something progressive that many liberal Christians could embrace.

As long as we remain within the binary of Christ and Satan, even if we behave like Christ, we are still defining ourselves as 'not Satan' and thereby still being defined by Satan and our relationship to Satan. It is only by stepping outside of the binary entirely that we can ever truly be free of Satan's shadow and darkness.

Before we all start getting carried away, thinking we have banished Satan once and for all and are about to achieve nirvana for ourselves, we might want to pause and remember that Jemisin's vision is a possible future which might be far harder to achieve than it is to describe. Far, far harder. Perhaps impossible. Perhaps we have been naïve or are in denial. Do we really think that we can set aside all selfishness and truly value all difference? Even when that difference works against our own self-interest? Really? Well, we can give it a try perhaps, but will we ever be able to convince every single human to behave in that very same fashion? As long as individuals have free will and independent thought, it's likely to be impossible.

So perhaps Satan's game isn't up, after all. He has an infinite number of tricks up his sleeve, besides. It would be just like him to convince us that he has been completely done away with, so that he can all the better catch us by surprise later, or so that he can continue to manipulate us all unwitnessed and blame-free. Then, Jemisin's post-Christian vision would simply be working as one of Satan's cunning lies.

It seems, then, that the Dark Lord might well return. We will begin to miss him, otherwise. There is something about his wickedness that delights us, after all. And he is such a colourful character that life would be a bit dull without him around, wouldn't it? Banish him forever more? Where would be the fun in that? At some point we will want to stop being so worthy, serious and dull. We will yearn for the sort of mischief we used to get up to before with our friend urging us on. Yes, it is against the rules and all good sense, but we did have a devil of a good time.

Thus, even when there is no Dark Lord in the narrative of SFF, as per Jemisin's books, we are perhaps doomed never to be free of him. He is a defining aspect of our cultural identity, after all. He will always return, no matter how many 'constructivist' (WNET Education, 2004) works like Jemisin's emerge or different constructivist approaches to SFF are shared.

It seems his return is inevitable. And that might well explain why there have been increasing calls within the fantasy readership for a return to the conservative days of 'epic fantasy'. The socio-political context, after all, has seen the US elect a right-wing Trump government and the UK opt for a Brexit led by a Conservative government. At the same time, populations across Europe have elected more right-wing governments. In 2016, when the West embraced such conservatism, a number of US and UK SFF conventions had panel debates on 'epic fantasy', a number of mainstream publishers (HarperVoyager included) had open submissions requesting 'epic fantasy' novels and personally I had fans emailing me to ask why there wasn't more 'epic fantasy' around (Dalton, 2017a).

The return of 'epic fantasy' would be a retrograde step in so many ways, even though it is easy to understand why people would yearn for a return of the reassuring and simpler 'golden age' of fantasy. They want to see hope and the virtuously heroic Chosen One restored. Yet they are calling for a sub-genre which traditionally offers hope only to a certain few, a sub-genre which works to ensure the political power within society remains with the traditional white elites and those invested in a hetero-normative patriarchy.

Yet, 'epic fantasy' will not return and be just as it was. The world has already internalised, understood and moved beyond it. Therefore, it cannot be the sole, dominant and all-defining sub-genre that it once was. It may be returning, but it can only do so as a conservative counterpoint to the liberalism of the likes of writers like Jemisin. Where elitist 'epic fantasy' insists upon traditional values, the 'post-fantasy' of authors like Jemisin continues to insist upon the essential importance of tolerance, resistance and protest. Societies now are more polarised and fraught than ever before, constantly plagued by subversion, assertion and reversion.

Polarised. Between and aggressive conservatism and an equally aggressive liberalism. Indeed, the polarisation is such that we are caught within a binary, just as we ever were. It's the same old binary of good and evil, Christ and Satan, white and black, male and female. We haven't escaped it, then, despite the best efforts and tolerance of the likes of Jemisin.

And the binary is more pernicious than ever, as each pole accuses the other of being the wrong-doer. Where does the truth lie? In a heated debate about what values are best for society, there are no facts. There are only personal opinions, personal objections, personal offence, rejections, accusations about false information and 'fake news'. In the absence of facts, there is no objectivity. There is only subjectivity and self-interest. In such a world, Satan can never be defeated and shut out, because it is impossible to identify precisely who is become Satan amongst us. In such a world, we can never shut him out of ourselves.

Finally, in terms of the longer game, the process of polarisation serves as a weapon in Satan's war against humankind and God. It is a puissant weapon that has successfully turned God's creation into a land of confusion and chaos. And we are creatures of that confusion and chaos. In becoming thus, we have (unwittingly) become part of the fight against God. Sadly, it will be our undoing.

Is there any hope or salvation left? God is all-knowing. He knows that we have been manipulated and that often we have acted unwittingly. He is all merciful. Let us pray He will forgive us our ignorance. Surely He will… if we are truly repentant. Here, ultimately, is where SFF will prove its absolute value, for SFF always intelligently explored our relationship with the world and God's creation. It has reflected sadly upon failed social and political systems, spelt out new philosophies, extrapolated into the future and provided new narratives about how we might improve ourselves. Always, SFF has sought ways for humankind to be better, more enlightened and more worthy. There has always been a positive humanism and spirituality underpinning SFF.

Always, its intentions and endeavour have been virtuous. And therein God will see there is something in us that might be saved. SFF will prove to be our salvation.

6. The author's Satanic end-note

If you are of a particular religious bent or persuasion, then you will believe that each of us has an individual and therefore unique relationship with God. By the same token, you might then believe each of us has an individual relationship with Satan. Indeed, as far as each of us can be considered individual or unique, each of us might be tempted or seduced differently by Satan, depending upon your individual weakness(es). If Satan *is* a part of each of us, as recent SFF has described, it is as a part of a uniquely different individual and as a part of the individual's unique difference. Thus, in some respects, the Satanic is perhaps *what makes each of us different and individual*. It is precisely because of such a line of thinking that I would – as the author of a book that has worked to describe the changing and affecting nature of the Satanic – like to share (or confess) some more *personal* musings and experiences that I have concerning the Satanic. They might help to provide some enlightenment or insights with regard to i) my own relationship with Satan, ii) my own 'take' on the Satanic and SFF and iii) the stance and possible partiality of my argument within this book. Ultimately, I am conscious that my own (unique) relationship with, (individual) experience of, and (personal) perspective upon the nature of the Satanic will in some way have 'coloured' my argument and description and will in some inevitable ways have been the self-indulgent *subject* of this book. In an attempt to aid your *objective* consideration as a reader, I will declare here some personal reflections, life-experiences and subjective preferences so that you can more easily "separate the fact from the fiction" in this book.

I have, for as long as I can remember, pondered a particular scenario or fantasy. Imagine that you were going to host a big party and that you could invite either Christ or Satan to attend. Who would you choose if you wanted the party to go off with a bang? Would you choose Christ? Wouldn't he just stand in a corner talking softly to a few of his dull but worthy followers while drinking a cup of tea? (Yes, he might be able to turn water into wine, but what self-respecting party is actually going to run out of wine and genuinely require this otherwise mildly diverting trick?). Or are you going to choose Satan, who would be the life of the party, have your friends howling with laughter and dancing with wild abandonment? There is something unapologetically attractive, exciting and uninhibited about Satan that means every party-host would have him top of their invite-list, even if the police and fire services usually end up being called at the end of the night or in the small hours of the morning. In this scenario, Satan is the brightest and most engaging of socialites, the funniest and most entrancing, the most outrageous and glamorous, the most wickedly self-centred and seductive… and, in being 'the most', is the most distinct and individual of us all.

On balance, I think I would invite Satan to my party. I often admire those who are free of inhibition and who behave with great individuality, especially in this class-ridden, overly mannered and socially restrictive UK of ours. Maybe it's because I was raised by a French mother who always found the British to be a bit stuffy or disapproving. Or maybe it was because I was sent to a High Church primary school which, although it provided a good education, was quite puritanical when it came to enforcing acceptable behaviour and punishing excessive displays of individuality. I rebelled young at that school, and have never regretted it, despite the problems it caused me… and has continued to cause me. How can I regret a certain strength of character… even if it is sometimes a weakness more than a strength?

Perhaps to escape, but certainly in the name of escapism, I was reading fantasy very early on, starting with Enid Blyton's *Adventures of the Wishing-Chair*. Even though it was YA fiction, the evil headmaster in it was as dark a Dark Lord as you'll find in any grimdark tale. I read Raymond Feist's *Magician* at the age of 15, and that got me hooked on 'epic fantasy', although Feist having the magician's apprentice Pug as a Chosen One always made me think of Mickey Mouse in the Disney movie of *Fantasia*. It was too cartoonish and bright. It felt forced, propagandist and not properly representative of the dark, Cold-War reality in which I was growing up.

I passed my Oxford University entrance exam, but my interviewers informed my school that I had 'an attitude problem'. So, I studied at the University of Warwick instead. I found I preferred the dark plays of Christopher Marlowe (*Doctor Faustus*, *The Jew of Malta*, etc) to the work of Shakespeare. I found I preferred the gothic styling and philosophy of Edgar Allan Poe to the realism of Upton Sinclair and the social satire of F. Scott Fitzgerald.

And so I found what I wanted to write. I coined the term 'metaphysical fantasy' as a term describing a sub-genre of literature in January 2008, when I established the www. metaphysicalfantasy.wordpress.com   (www.ajdalton.eu) website to coincide with the release of my self-published novel *Necromancer's Gambit* in February 2008. The novel bore a gold badge on the cover declaring it 'The best of Metaphysical Fantasy'. I coined the term for two main reasons: i) as a marketing ploy, via which I would 'own' a new sub-genre and ii) as a way of distinguishing the novel as offering something new and distinct to the wider genre. Before making the costly[1] decision to self-publish, I had submitted *Necromancer's Gambit* to every major publisher of fantasy, but had been universally rejected with statements including 'It's too dark' and 'It doesn't fit squarely within the genre'[2]. Ironically, the book's own originality and difference from the *norm* within the genre was considered its weakness by the leading publishers.

In 2011, based on both the considerable sales of *The Flesh & Bone Trilogy* (of which *Necromancer's Gambit* was the first title) and the 'freshness'[3] offered by 'metaphysical fantasy', Gollancz, the UK's leading publisher of fantasy and sci-fi, gave me a three-book deal for *Chronicles of a Cosmic Warlord*. *Empire of the Saviours*, the first title in *Chronicles of a Cosmic Warlord*, was published in the UK in 2012, was sold into Blanvalet (Random House) in Germany in 2012, and was long-listed for the BFS National Fantasy Award (The Gemmell Award) in 2013. All this marked the arrival (and ultimate acceptance) of 'metaphysical fantasy' within the pantheon of established sub-genres of fantasy literature.

'Metaphysical fantasy' emerged specifically in the mid to late 2000s, at a time when the UK was experiencing economic, political, social and moral turmoil. In such a context, the Chosen One, class structure, judgemental morality and social stability of the 'epic fantasy' kingdom were exposed as redundant and/or false. What 'metaphysical

---

1. In this pre-Kindle era, self-publishing was far from a cheap option – I paid £2000 to AuthorHouse to see *Necromancer's Gambit* 'published', placed in Waterstones stores and represented on book-selling websites.

2. References are commercial-in-confidence.

3. An email from Marcus Gipps, commissioning editor at Gollancz, to A J Dalton, August 2008.

fantasy' offered instead was a psychologically fraught protagonist (anti-hero), social change, a moral ambivalence and the tolerance of difference. In doing so, 'metaphysical fantasy' laid the foundations for the subsequent second-world fantasy sub-genre of 'grimdark fantasy', a sub-genre which presents a survivalist as protagonist, an expedient sense of morality, uncompromising behaviours and extreme outrage.

Second-world fantasy has come a very long way since the days of the original British 'high fantasy' of Tolkien's *The Lord of the Rings*. Where 'high fantasy' tends to offer an omniscient narrator, a singular and epic worldview, Christian values, a Satanic antagonist, a Christ-like Chosen One and a lack of irony, 'metaphysical fantasy' presents us with a plurality of narrative points of view, a subversion of religious doctrine, ambiguous and inconstant characters, and plenty of irony and dark humour. Indeed, the 'problem' of religion and the theme of competing philosophies of being is more distinct in 'metaphysical fantasy' than in any other sub-genre to date. In this sense, 'metaphysical fantasy' could be described as the first 'post-Christian' sub-genre of fantasy, its ultimate concern not the prescription of particular social behaviours but a philosophical consideration of the individual's place in the cosmos. 'Metaphysical fantasy' does not presume to provide answers to its consideration, describing a more modern (Millennial) experience than 'epic fantasy'. Unlike later 'grimdark fantasy', however, 'metaphysical fantasy' tends to culminate optimistically with an understanding of the importance of friendship, fidelity and knowledge of others, tolerating challenge and difference, and celebrating subversive humour and the courage to act.

Where the self-published but best-selling *Necromancer's Gambit* began the development of 'metaphysical fantasy', I would say *Empire of the Saviours* (which gained so much international recognition) truly focussed and best articulated the themes, relevance, motifs, characterisation, plot and literary style of 'metaphysical fantasy'. *Empire of the Saviours* was the book that finally established the distinct and valuable contribution of 'metaphysical fantasy' to the wider fantasy genre. Indeed, it was following the publication of *Empire of the Saviours* that other authors began to publish work using or described by the label of 'metaphysical fantasy', including Neil Gaiman[4], Taya Wood (2009), Jim Murdoch (2015), Robin Coe (2010), James Riley (Swinyard, 2016), David Lindsay (Valentine, 2015), and the list goes on.

> Beware those who speak of faith and the betterment
> of the people yet say magic is the work of the devil.
> (Dalton, 2012, p. v)

---

4. *American Gods: The Tenth Anniversary Edition: A Novel* on www. amazon.co.uk is categorised under and tagged with 'Metaphysical & Visionary' fantasy.

7. Bibliography

A&C Black, 1935. *Who's Who?*. [online] Available at: <http://archive.org/stream/whoswho1935001355mbp#page/n7> [Accessed: 19 August 2018].

Abercrombie, J., 2006. *The Blade Itself: The First Law*. London: Gollancz.

Albrecht, M., 1956. Does literature reflect common values?. *American Sociological Review*, 21(6), pp. 722-729, [Online] Available at: <https://www.jstor.org/stable/2088424?seq=1#page_scan_tab_contents> [Accessed: 3 November 2017].

Alexander, L., 1971. High Fantasy and Heroic Romance. [online] Available at: <http://www.hbook.com/1971/12/choosing-books/horn-book-magazine/high-fantasy-and-heroic-romance/> [Accessed: 3 November 2017].

Bakker, R. S., 2004. *The Darkness That Comes Before*. London: Orbit.

BBC, 2016. *Frankenstein and the Vampyre: A Dark and Stormy Night*. [online] Available at: <https://www.bbc.co.uk/programmes/b04nvq7q> [Accessed: 1 August 2019].

BBC4, 2018. *Mark Kermode's Secrets of Cinema: Science Fiction*. [online] Available at: <https://www.bbc.co.uk/programmes/b0bf7wrl> [Accessed: 18 August 2018].

Beard, H. and Kenney, D., 1969. *Bored of the Rings*. New York: Touchstone.

Beauvais, V., 2018. *Speculum Historiale*. [online] Available at: <http://www.vincentiusbelvacensis.eu> [Accessed: 14 March 2018].

Benoît Eyriès, J., 1812. *Fantasmagoriana*. Paris: F. Schoell.

Biblica, 1978. *Holy Bible: New International Version*. London: Hodder & Stoughton.

Blake, W., 1808. Jerusalem. In: *Milton: A Poem in Two Books*. London: William Blake.

Brett, P. V., 2008. *The Painted Man: The Demon Cycle*. London: Voyager Books.

Bronte, C., 1849. *Shirley*. Yorkshire: Smith, Elder & Co.

Campbell, A., 2006. *Scar Night*. New York: Tor.

Campbell, C., 1949. *The Hero with a Thousand Faces*. USA: Pantheon Books.

Carpenter, H., 1977. *J. R. R. Tolkien: A Biography*. New York: Ballantine Books.

Carpenter, H. and Tolkien, C. (eds.), 1981. *The Letters of J. R. R. Tolkien*. London: George Allen & Unwin.

Child, B., 2016. *Not the future after all: the slow demise of young adult dystopian sci-fi films*. The Guardian, [Online] 25 March. Available at: <https://www.theguardian.com/film/2016/mar/25/allegiant-young-adult-dystopian-films-box-office-flops> [Accessed: 10 November 2017].

Clute, J. and Grant, J., 1997. *The Encyclopedia of Fantasy*. London: Orbit.

Coe, R., 2010. 'Robin Coe', *Twitter*. [online] Available at: www.twitter.com/robin_coe> [Accessed: 12 July 2016].

Collins, S., 2008. *The Hunger Games*. New York: Scholastic Press.

Dalton, A. J., 2012. *Empire of the Saviours: Book One: Chronicles of a Cosmic Warlord*. London: Gollancz.

Dalton, A. J. (2013). George RR Martin and Tolkien have a lot to answer for. [online] Available at: <http://www.scifinow.co.uk/blog/38508/

fantasy-author-a-j-dalton-asks-why-do-we-all-sound-like-george-rr-martin/> [Accessed: 19 August 2018].

Dalton, A. J., 2017a. Gender identity and sexuality in current sub-genres of British fantasy literature. In: Barbini, F. (ed.). 2017. *Gender Identity and Sexuality in Current Fantasy and Science Fiction*. Edinburgh: Luna Press Publishing, pp. 57-81.

Dalton, A. J., 2008a. *Metaphysical Fantasy*. [online] Available at: <www.ajdalton.eu> [Accessed: 15 July 2016].

Dalton, A. J., 2016. New trends in Fantasy and SciFi. *Gollancz*, [online] Available at: <https://www.gollancz.co.uk/2016/11/new-trends-in-fantasy-and-scifi-a-guest-post-by-aj-dalton/> [Accessed: 11 November 2017].

Dalton, A. J., 2009. *Necromancer's Betrayal: Book Two of The Flesh & Bone Trilogy*. Milton Keynes: AuthorHouse UK.

Dalton, A. J., 2010. *Necromancer's Fall: Book Three of The Flesh & Bone Trilogy*. Milton Keynes: AuthorHouse UK.

Dalton, A. J., 2008b. *Necromancer's Gambit: Book One of The Flesh & Bone Trilogy*. Milton Keynes: AuthorHouse UK.

Dalton, A. J., 2017b. *The Sub-genres of British Fantasy Literature*. Edinburgh: Luna Press Publishing.

Dalton, A. J., 2014. *Tithe of the Saviours: Book Three: Chronicles of a Cosmic Warlord*. London: Gollancz.

Dashner, J., 2009. *The Maze Runner*. New York: Delacorte Press.

Di Filippo, P., 1995. *The Steampunk Trilogy*. New York: Four Walls Eight Windows.

Dickens, C., 1854. *Hard Times*. London: Bradbury and Evans.

Donaldson, S., 1986a. *Mordant's Need*. New York: Del Ray Books.

Donaldson, S., 1986b. *Epic Fantasy in the Modern World: A Few Observations*. Ohio: Kent State University Libraries.

Donaldson, S., 1977a. *Lord Foul's Bane: An Epic Fantasy*. New York: Holt, Rinehart and Winston.

Donaldson, S., 1977b. *The Power that Preserves*. New York: Holt, Rinehart and Winston.

Dozois, G., 1997. *Modern Classics of Fantasy*. New York: St. Martin's Press.

Dracula, 2013. [TV series]. NBC, 25 October.

Eddings, D., 1982. *Pawn of Prophecy*. New York: Del Rey Books.

Elliott, L., 2011. Britain's richest 5% gained most from quantitative easing – Bank of England. *The Guardian*, [Online] 23 August. Available at: <https://www.theguardian.com/business/2012/aug/23/britains-richest-gained-quantative-easing-bank> [Accessed: 10 November 2017].

Feist, R., 1986. *A Darkness at Sethanon*. New York: Doubleday.

Feist, R., 1982. *Magician*. New York: Doubleday.

Freud, S., 1899. *The Interpretation of Dreams*. Leipzig and Vienna: Franz Deuticke.

Freud, S. and Breuer, J., 1895. *Studies on Hysteria*. Leipzig and Vienna: Franz Deuticke.

Gaiman, N., 1996. *Neverwhere*. London: BBC Books.

Gaiman, N., n. d. Neverwhere. [online] Available at: <http://www.neilgaiman.com/works/Books/Neverwhere/> [Accessed: 12 July 2016].

Game of Thrones, 2011. [TV series]. HBO, 17 April.

Gödel, K., 1931. Über formal unentscheidbare Sätze der Principia Mathematica und verwandter Systeme: I. *Monatshefte für Mathematik und Physik*, 38(1), pp. 173–198.

Goodkind, T., 1994. *Wizard's First Rule*. New York: Tor Fantasy.

Gothic, 1986. [film] Directed by Ken Russell. UK: Virgin Vision.

Groom, N., 2014. *Horace Walpole: The Castle of Otranto*. New York: Oxford University Press.

Hampson, F., 1950. 'Dan Dare'. *The Eagle*. London: Hulton Press.

Hughes, M., 2003. *John Milton: Paradise Lost*. Cambridge: Hackett Publishing Company.

Hunt, S., 1994. *For the Crown and the Dragon*. London: Green Nebula Publishing.

James, E., 2012. Tolkien, Lewis and the explosion of genre fantasy, in James, E. and Mendlesohn, F. (eds.) *The Cambridge Companion to Fantasy Literature*. Cambridge: Cambridge University Press, pp. 62-78.

Jemisin, N. K., 2015. *The Fifth Season: Book One: The Broken Earth Trilogy*. New York: Orbit.

Jeter, K., 1979. *Morlock Night*. London: Duncan Baird Publishers.

Jeter, K., 1987. Science Fiction Citations. [online] Available at: <http://www.jessesword.com/sf/view/327> [Accessed: 11 July 2016].

Jones, J. V., 1995. *The Baker's Boy*. New York: Aspect.
Kant, I., 1781. *Critique of Pure Reason*. Riga: J. F. Hartknoch.

Kaveney, R., 2012. Dark fantasy and paranormal romance, in James, E. and Mendlesohn, F. (eds.) *The Cambridge Companion to Fantasy*

Literature. Cambridge: Cambridge University Press, pp. 214-223.

Kelly, H. A., 2006. *Satan: A Biography*. Cambridge: Cambrige University Press.

Kline, A., 2018a. *Geoffrey Chaucer: The Canterbury Tales*. [online] Available at: <https://www.poetryintranslation.com/PITBR/English/Canthome.php#highlighttroilus+and+criseyde> [Accessed: 28 March 2018].

Kline, A., 2018b. *Geoffrey Chaucer: Troilus and Criseyde*. [online] Available at: <https://www.poetryintranslation.com/PITBR/English/Chaucerhome.php> [Accessed: 28 March 2018].

Komarck, M., 2015. *In Defence of the Chosen One*. [online] Available at: <http://fantasy-faction.com/2015/in-defence-of-the-chosen-one> [Accessed: 11 July 2016].

Lawrence, M., 2011. *Prince of Thorns: The Broken Empire Trilogy*. London: HarperCollins UK.

Lévi-Strauss, C., 1955. The structural study of myth. *The Journal of American Folklore*, 68(270), pp. 428-444.

Lewis, C. S., 1950. *The Lion, the Witch and the Wardrobe*. London: Bles.

Lord Byron, 1813. *The Giaour*. London: John Murray.

True Blood, 2008. [TV Series]. HBO, 7 September.

Lucifer, 2016. [TV series]. Fox Broadcasting Company, 25 January.

Marlowe, C., 2003. *Doctor Faustus*. [online] Available at: https://manybooks.net/book/125374/read#epubcfi(/6/8[html1]!/4/160/1:9) [Accessed: 1 August 2019].

McPherson, B., 2001-13. *Hell in the Old Testament*. [online] Available at: <http://www.biblestudying.net/cosmo-5> [Accessed: 1 March 2018].

Melville, H., 1851. *Moby-Dick*. London: Richard Bentley.

Mendlesohn, F., 2008. *Rhetorics of Fantasy*. Connecticut: Wesleyan University Press.

Mendlesohn, F. and James, E., 2009. *A Short History of Fantasy*. London: Middlesex University Press.

Metropolis, 1927. [film] Directed by Fritz Lang. Germany: UFA.

Meyer, S., 2008. *Breaking Dawn*. New York: Little, Brown and Co.

Meyer, S., 2007. *Eclipse*. New York: Little, Brown and Co.

Meyer, S., 2006. *New Moon*. New York: Little, Brown and Co.

Meyer, S., 2005. *Twilight*. New York: Little, Brown and Co.

Modesitt Jr., L. E., 1991. *The Magic of Recluce*. Charlotte, NC: Paw Prints.

Moorcock, M., 1970. *The Eternal Champion*. New York: Dell Books.

Moorcock, M., 1974. *The Hollow Lands*. New York: Harper and Row.

Moorcock, M., 1987. *Wizardry and Wild Romance: A Study of Epic Fantasy*. London: Gollancz.

Murdoch, J., 2015. *What is Metaphysical Fantasy?* [online] Available at: <www.jmurdoch.com/what-is-metaphysical-fantasy> [Accessed: 12 July 2016].

Niven, L., 1970. *Ringworld*. New York: Ballantine Books.

Pratchett, T., 2011. *Snuff*. New York: Doubleday.

Prynne, W., 1632. *Histriomastix*. London: Michael Sparke.

Raif, S., 2013. Police sergeant jailed for selling information to the Sun newspaper. *The Independent*, [Online] 9 May. Available at: <http://www.independent.co.uk/news/uk/ crime/police-sergeant-jailed-for-selling-information-to-the-sun-newspaper-8608989.html> [Accessed: 1 December 2017].

Reagan, R., 1983. 'Evil empire', speech at 41st Annual Convention. National Association of Evangelicals. Unpublished.

Renner, R., 2010. *A Light in Darkness Vol.1*. Tulsa, Oklahoma: Harrison House Publishers.

Roth, C., 1971. *Encyclopaedia Judaica*. Jerusalem: Keter Publishing House.

Senior, W., 1995. *Variations on the Fantasy Tradition: Stephen R. Donaldson's Chronicles of Thomas Covenant*. Ohio: The Kent State University Press.

Senior, W. A., 2012. Quest Fantasies. In: E. James and F. Mendlesohn (eds.). 2012. *The Cambridge Companion to Fantasy Literature*. New York: Cambridge University Press.

Shelley, M., 1818. *Frankenstein: The Modern Prometheus*. London: Lackington, Hughes, Harding, Mavor, & Jones.

Sherwood, H., 2016a. Church of England weekly attendance falls below 1m for first time. *The Guardian*, [Online] 12 January. Available at: <https://www.theguardian.com/world/2016/jan/12/church-of-england-attendance-falls-below-million-first-time> [Accessed: 14 March 2018].

Sherwood, H., 2016b. People of no religion outnumber Christians. *The Guardian*, [Online] 23 May. Available at: <https://www.theguardian.com/world/2016/may/23/no-religion-outnumber-christians-england-wales-study> [Accessed: 14 March 2018].

Smith, A. G., 2010. *Lockdown: Escape from Furnace*. New York: Tor.

Soars, J. and Soars, L., 1987. *Headway: Upper-intermediate*. Oxford: Oxford University Press.

Société des Bollandistes, 1895. *Bibliotheca Hagiographica Graeca*. Bruxelles: Apud editories.

Stableford, B., 2005. *The A to Z of Fantasy Literature*. Plymouth: Scarecrow Press.

Stevenson, R., 1886. *The Strange Case of Dr Jekyll and Mr Hyde*. London: Longmans, Green and Co.

Stoker, B., 1897. *Dracula*. London: Archibald Constable and Co.

Swinyard, H., 2016. '#MetaphysicalFantasy', *Twitter*, 9 January. [online] Available at: <www.twitter.com/search?q=%Metaphysicalfantasy&src=typd> [Accessed: 12 July 2016].

Terry Pratchett Books, 2011. Snuff – third fastest selling novel since records began! [online] Available at: <https://www.terrypratchettbooks.com/snuff-third-fastest-selling-novel-since-records-began/> [Accessed: 1 August 2019].

The Book Plank, 2014. *Author Interview with Stephen Hunt*. [online] Available at: <http://thebookplank.blogspot.co.uk/2014/05/author-interview-with-stephen-hunt.html> [Accessed: 15 July 2016].

The Caffeinated Symposium, 2011. Fantasy: 1990-2000: *The Age of the Doorstops and Gimmicks*. [online] Available at: <http://caffeinesymposium.blogspot.co.uk/2011/07/fantasy-1990-2000-age-of-doorstops-and.html> [Accessed: 15 July 2016].

Tolkien, J. R. R., 1954-55. *The Lord of the Rings*. London: Allen & Unwin.

Tolkien, J. R. R., and Tolkien, C. (ed.), 1977. *The Silmarillion*. London: George Allen and Unwin.

Tolkien, J. R. R., and Tolkien, C. (ed.), 1993. *Morgoth's Ring*. Boston: Houghton Mifflin, p. 52.

Tolkien, J. R. R., 1954a. *The Fellowship of the Ring: Being the First Part of The Lord of the Rings*. London: George Allen & Unwin.

Tolkien, J. R. R., 1955. *The Return of the King: Being the Third Part of The Lord of the Rings*. London: George Allen & Unwin.

Tolkien, J. R. R., 1954b. *The Two Towers: Being the Second Part of The Lord of the Rings*. London: George Allen & Unwin.

Tolkien, J. R. R., 1937. *The Hobbit, or There and Back Again*. London: George Allen & Unwin.

Treanor, J., 2011. RBS bankers get £950m in bonuses despite £1.1bn loss. *The Guardian*, [Online] 24 February. Available at: <https://www.theguardian.com/business/2011/feb/24/rbs-bankers-bonuses-despite-loss> [Accessed: 10 November 2017].

True Blood, 2008. [TV Series]. HBO, 7 September.

Valentine, M., 2015. *The Universal Witch*. [online] Available at: <www.wormwoodiana.blogspot.co.uk/2015_10_01_archive.html> [Accessed: 12 July 2016].

Voragine, J., 2003. *The Golden Legend*. London: Aeterna Press.
Walpole, H., 1764. *The Castle of Otranto: A Gothic Story*. London: William Bathoe.

Wells, H. G., 1895. *The Time Machine*. London: William Heinemann.
Wells, H. G., 1898. The War of the Worlds. London: William Heinemann.

WNET Education, 2004. Constructivism as a Paradigm for Teaching and Learning. [online] Available at: <https://www.thirteen.org/edonline/concept2class/constructivism/index.html> [Accessed: 14 August 2019].

Wolfe, G., 2005. Coming to terms, in Gunn, J. and Candelaria, M. (eds.) *Speculations on Speculation: Theories of Science Fiction*. Maryland: Scarecrow Press Inc, pp.13-22.

Wolfe, G., 2011. *Evaporating Genres: Essays on Fantastic Literature*. Connecticut: Wesleyan University Press.

Wood, T., 2009. 'Taya Wood', *Twitter*. [online] Available at: <www. twitter.com/tayawood> [Accessed: 12 July 2016].

Wyndham, J., 1951. *The Day of the Triffids*. London: Michael Joseph.

Wyndham, J., 1957. *The Midwich Cuckoos*. London: Michael Joseph.

Young, J., 2005. Terry Pratchett on the Origins of Discworld, His Order of the British Empire and Everything in between. *Science Fiction Weekly*, 449.